WILDERNESS TO WASHINGTON

An 1811 Journey on Horseback

by

Eleanor Rice Long

For information write:
Reflections Press
a division of T.I.S. Enterprises
P.O. Box 1998
Bloomington, Indiana 47402

Library of Congress Catalog Card No.   81-51895
ISBN 0-89917-324-1

To Newell and Ed who have always given me the best of everything.

JONATHAN JENNINGS

The charismatic young lawyer from Pennsylvania came to the Indiana Territory to seek his political fortune and found his great love, the brave and beautiful

ANN GILMORE HAY

Raised a "lady" in Kentucky and still in her teen-years, Ann would become the first congressman's wife to accompany her husband across a thousand miles of wilderness to be at his side while he served in the Congress of 1811. An excellent horsewoman, she rode her beloved mare

GINGER

This spunky little horse carried her mistress through endless forests, across rivers and mountains and unfriendly Indian camps, following the steady leadership of

BIG BROWN

The great stallion proved to be as powerful and sturdy a horse as had ever carried a devoted master through adventure and romance.

This is a fictionalized story of two real people who actually made such a journey. Thorough research gives authenticity to the historical background and plausibility to the imagined adventures.

I

A Wondrous Beginning Day

It was no ordinary day in the life of Ann Gilmore Hay, the most beautiful and popular belle in the whole Indiana Territory. This very morning she would become Madame Jonathan Jennings, bride of the handsome young lawyer come from Pennsylvania to seek his political fortune, newly-elected delegate to the Congress of the United States in this year of 1811.

From the cottonwood trees outside the girl's window came the bird songs of early dawn, yet Ann lay quite still in the great canopied bed. Her long hair lay spread like an open fan across her pillow. Her small body made only the slightest bulge under the handwoven coverlet warming her against the early chill of August.

Yet the young girl was not sleeping. Her brown eyes stared wide. Only her nose wrinkled as she sniffed the delicious aroma of spices from sweet hams roasting in the summer kitchen.

From below came the sounds of a household busy with preparations for her wedding day when suddenly, the girl turned her face into the down of her pillow and pulled the coverlet over her head. Her body shook with muffled sobs.

Just then the door of the girl's room was slowly opened. The squeaking hinges warned Ann and she sat up quickly as her mother entered. Ann hastily brushed away her tears.

"So ye be awake, sleepy one! Sure it be a beautiful marryin' day for ye now," and Ann's mother moved to stroke the reddish-brown hair so like her own. "Why, Ann-daughter, ye've been cryin'! Tears on your weddin' morn?"

Ann flung her arms about her mother. "O Mama, I'm fearful of this day."

"Why, my dear Ann? Is it the journey ridin' the wilderness to Washington City that ye be fearin'?"

"It's not the journey, Mama. I'll be riding the best mare in the whole Territory and Jonathan has made the way before. It's the leaving you and my brothers and sisters. Why I've never been once away. And you do be needing me now that Papa's died. I'd best not be marrying at all, ever."

"Nonsense, Daughter. It be the best way of life with the right one to be sharin'. But I do not like the journeyin' for ye, to be sure. No road to be followin' and the trails full of dangers!"

"It's more fearful of Washington City, I'll be—meeting important people and all. I would not want Jonathan to be ashamed ever."

"Now, Daughter, remember ye've been raised a lady. To be yourself will be plenty good enough, I be thinkin'." Then Mama Hay sighed. "But whoever heard tell of a congressman's wife not yet turned twenty."

At that moment they heard the sound of horses' hoofs pounding up the hill. Ann slid from the high bed and ran to the window.

"Whoa! Whoa, Boy! Easy, Big Brown!" A great spirited horse pawed the air with strong forelegs. The young rider dismounted eagerly and tossed the reins to the stable boy who came running to meet him. The rider doffed his hat and looked up to Ann's window. The bridegroom had come to claim his bride.

Ann's mother pulled her back. "It be bad fortune for the bride and groom to be seein' each other afore the pledgin' of their marryin' vows."

Ann danced across the room. "I'll be following my wonderful Jonathan J. through the wilderness, across the mountains, for better, for worse, for whatever forever."

"So ye've decided to be marryin' after all, have ye?" laughed Mama Hay. "But ye won't be followin' at all if ye not be settlin' down to make ready. Here's Becky come to help. I'll be seein' to our guests arrivin'."

Becky was breathing heavily climbing up the steep stairway. "Miz Ann, honey, I hates you goin' away."

"Don't be fretting, dear Becky. I'll be coming back at the close of the Congress, you know."

"Hummph—Indians and wild animals and the likes. And who foods you and takes keer o' your needs, Miz Ann? You's been my baby."

"There'll be friendly cabins along the way. Mister Jennings says there be so many settlements now in Ohio Territory that it's been made a state already."

At the sound of horses and wagons pulling up the hill, Becky hurried to the window. "Guests be a comin'. Guests be a comin'." Ann hastened to make ready for her wedding.

She was soon dressed in Jonathan's favorite white, carrying a bouquet of late summer roses just as she had the day Jonathan had fallen in love with her. At last Becky was satisfied that every tiny fold was in place. The magic moment had arrived.

Ann ran eagerly to the head of the stairs but when she looked down and saw Jonathan waiting for her, standing so handsome and dignified in his new clothes, she stopped abruptly. When she stepped forth again, it was with the careful dignity as should become the bride of a congressman.

When the Indians had moved north to new hunting grounds, Ann's father had come to Kentucky to help survey this new village of Charles Town. Many families had come to settle this beautiful land on the Ohio River and today it seemed that all were gathered in the parlor of the great log house Papa Hay had built for his family.

The perfume of night-blooming stock mingled with the spicy odor of early fall marigolds as Jonathan's strong voice pledged his vows. Ann heard her own voice as if from afar promising to "love, honor, and obey." She stood on tiptoe to receive the kiss to seal their vows but Jonathan gathered his tiny bride into his arms and lifted her clear off the floor. The guests laughed and cheered. Only Mama and Becky brushed tears from their eyes.

But Becky's shiny black cheeks soon stretched into a proud smile as she and Mama Hay opened the doors to the dining room. There set lighter-than-air biscuits and the hickory-smoked hams Ann had smelled roasting in their spices. On the side-table stood two wedding cakes—a white one for the bride's cake and a dark spice cake for the groom's.

"I hope I get the ring," whispered Cousin Jane.

But it was Deborah who screamed, "I've got it! I've got the ring. I'll be the next bride."

"Who you-all goin' to marry, Miss Deborah?" and the boys pretended to run away from her.

"Let's catch her a husband," Ann called gaily.

"Not me," laughed Jonathan. "I'm just an old married man."

"Bother!" drawled Sadie. "Here's the old maid's thimble in my cake and me not sewing a stitch."

"You'd best be learning then," teased Charlie, "for I don' aim for you to be an old maid, Miss Sadie, and I'll be needin' mendin'."

3

"Mendin' what, Sir? A broken heart?"

"Look who's found the ha-penny! Ol' Doc Andrew, travelled all the way from Lexington Medical School for his sister's wedding. This'll fetch you luck with the girls, Sir, and you'll be needin' it, ol' saw-bones."

The boys strained and tugged on Andrew's boot until they had pulled it off and they put the ha-penny into the heel. Andrew recovered his boot and limped about the room chasing the girls.

Ann was at the center of all the fun when Jonathan led her aside. "It's time to be leaving, my little bride."

"O Jonathan, not yet! There'll be dancing at the Green Tree Tavern and celebrating all the rest of the day."

Ann was used to having her way but she noticed the sternness in Jonathan's face.

"Miss Ann, I have duties waiting. I have been elected to serve my country in the Congress and there are a thousand miles to ride."

Ann's smile vanished. So this was Master Jonathan Jennings the Congressman, she thought. Where was her "wonderful Jonathan J.?" Ann sighed. "It will take much learning to being a wife," but she spoke the words only to herself. She obeyed her husband and mounted lightly up the stairs, pausing only to blow him a kiss.

Becky followed. "Miz Ann, honey, I'm a comin' to help you change. They's already brung the horses round."

"O Becky, I can't tolerate having my wedding day come to an end."

"Nothin's comin' to an end, Miz Ann, chile. It's just bein' a wondrous beginnin' day."

"Please to try calling me 'Madame Jennings', Becky. I need to get used to the sound of it."

Sister Nancy stood curtsying at the door. "I'm minding my manners. You're wife to a congressman now."

"O Nancy, you're always the one for teasing. Come help undo me—all these tiny buttons."

"If those buttons were on me, I'd be poppin' 'em clear off cause I ate too many good victuals. O Sister, must you truly change from your weddin' dress? It becomes you so."

Ann sighed as she turned away from the mirror. "Can you imagine wearing it riding through the forests?" Both girls giggled.

4

"How I wish I could be taking it with me but I have only my saddlebags and they won't carry my beautiful dress. Here, Nancy, help Becky to pack it away. One day you may be wearing it for your marrying."

Nancy held the dress up to her own little-girl figure. She touched the dainty rows of tucks and embroideries and fingered the fine lace that a Scotch-Irish grandmother had brought all the way from Scotland. She paraded before the tall pier glass. Then suddenly she stamped her foot.

"I'll never be havin' a weddin'. Who'd ever marry up with me. All these freckles and my ugly red braids."

Becky spoke sharply. "Miz Nancy, don' you ever be stampin' your foot like that. It ain't becomin' in a lady."

"Don't be fretting, little Sister. You're growing up and you be prettier every day."

"Whatever will you wear for all the grand doings in Washington City? They won't be just plain old play-parties like here in Charles Town—real dress-up balls most likely," and Nancy began to swing and sway to her own humming, spreading her skirts and pirouetting about the room. "What wonderful tales you'll have to tell when you come home."

No one heard the girls' mother come up the stairs. Madame Hay stood at the door, watching as Becky helped Ann don the handsome riding clothes made especially for the horseback journey.

The long wrap-around skirt designed for riding sidesaddle was of sturdy linsey-woolsey, the color of earth. Mama Hay herself had spun the yarn and dyed the threads. She had strung the loom with the wool yarns lengthwise and moved her shuttle to carry the linen thread crosswise.

"Ann-daughter, ye may be buying more stylish clothes one day but none that become ye more."

Ann rushed to greet her. "My riding clothes are elegant, Mama. I'm proud to be wearing them."

"I wanted to weave cloth stout enough for the hazards of the trails. I chose the woods color to conceal ye from dangers in the forests. Here let me help ye," as Ann was fastening a golden locket.

"This beautiful gift from Jonathan, I shall wear till the day I die." The locket held a miniature portrait* of Jonathan Jennings whose strong face and kindly eyes the artist had caught so well.

"Mama has a gift for you, too," Nancy sang out. "I saw her put it in your saddle pouch."

"O Nancy! I wished to surprise your sister. It's only a small sum for fripperies and such, but we want our congressman's wife from the Indiana Territory to look as pretty as any of the fine ladies in Washington City."

"What's that about my sister looking pretty?" Brother Andrew stood at the door, ready to fetch Ann's things below. "Why our Miss Ann's bound to be the prettiest girl in the whole of Washington City."

Ann laughed delightedly. "Do you not forget I'm no longer a *girl*, Brother Andrew? I'm a married *lady* now."

As Andrew went ahead with the saddlebags, Ann gave a last loving hug to her mother, another to Nancy and Becky. Then with her feet scarcely touching the stair treads, she flew down the steps to her "wonderful Jonathan J."—and to Ginger.

Ann's father had given her the little mare when she was only a foal. "She's as sweet as Becky's gingerbread and the same color. I shall name her Ginger." The mare became her first love—until the day she met Jonathan Jennings, come to do political business with her father. "I had to turn away lest he see the wonder in my eyes," she confided to Becky. Now she was soon to be away with both loves on the biggest adventure of her life.

The guests gathered to see the bride and groom depart for the 1811 session of the Congress in Washington City.

"Whyever would they let Miss Ann go on such a dangerous journey?" one guest said to another. "And leavin' her Mama so soon after John Hay's death, I do declare."

"I never heard of such a business—such a young girl and all," as other guests joined in.

"I hear Miss Ann begged to be allowed to go and they say Mister Jennings can deny her nothing."

—

* A portrait made from this miniature of Jonathan Jennings, who became Indiana's first Governor, hangs today in the first State House in the town of Corydon, Indiana's first Capital.

"I think it's just too romantic," sighed another.

"Hummph! I wouldn't want to be in her boots, riding all that way, and what if she gets the ague or that beloved mare of hers goes lame?"

"Worse than that—it is said that there be mountains to be crossed with bears and brigands in them and there still be Indian camps in the Ohio Territory, ain't there?"

"O dear, you talk like we might never be seein' Miss Ann again and everybody lovin' her so."

"Fiddle-de-dee! With a husband like Mister Jennings to look out for her—oh, here she comes! Miss Ann—I mean Madame Jennings, you do look elegant. We be goin' to miss you."

"Yeah, who's going to Skip-to My-Lou at the Green Tree tonight?" called Cousin Charlie. "Nobody can do-si-do like you, Miss Ann."

Amidst cries of Godspeed and waving of handkerchiefs, the bride and groom mounted their horses. They rode off in an eager gallop, but once out of sight, Ann slowed Ginger and turned in her saddle to look back.

"What's the matter, Miss Ann? Have you left something behind?"

"Indeed now, we left all the fun and celebrating behind. There'll be dancing and singing and teasing this night. I'm wishing we could have stayed for the play-party for our own marrying."

"You'll be dancing in the elegant houses in the Capital one day—maybe even in the President's Palace, but not if we don't keep on our way." Then Jonathan hesitated. "Are you sorry you married me, Miss Ann—taking you away and all?"

"Being a wife will take some getting used to, I am thinking. But what are we dawdling for, Sir? Give your horse his head, Mister Jennings, and let's be off on our honeymoon-journey."

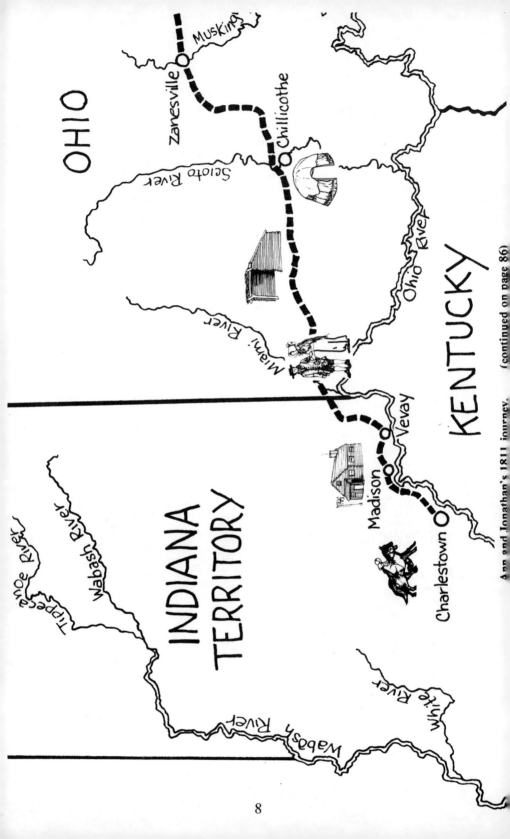

OHIO

Muskin[gum]

Zanesville

Chillicothe

Scioto River

Miami River

Ohio River

KENTUCKY

INDIANA TERRITORY

Wabash River

Tippecanoe River

White River

Wabash River

Madison

Vevay

Charlestown

Ann and Jonathan's 1811 journey,   (continued on page 86)

8

II

An Unexpected Welcome

At first the miles made for easy riding, even though the horses were heavily loaded with bulging saddlebags. Big Brown was a powerful stallion and had crossed the wilderness before when he carried Jonathan to serve his first elected term in the Congress. Ginger, however, was a small horse and had yet to prove equal to the rough journey that lay ahead.

Both horses were the same shade of brown and both held their heads high, until one looked like the proud shadow of the other.

Ann and Jonathan were excellent riders who held the respect of their horses. They rode side-by-side at first, but all too soon, the wagon road narrowed into a single-horse trail. Now both riders and horses must dodge low branches of ever-thickening woods where puddles often slowed the horses to a walk. Soon deep shadows engulfed them. The rays of the sun penetrated the tall trees in only occasional patterns of quivering light.

Then abruptly the woods thinned and the riders came to an open glade of green grasses beside a creek.

"We'd best rest the horses here where they can drink and find a spot of pasture. Come, Ann—us, too." And he led his bride to a broad sycamore tree standing white-trunked beside the sparkling waters of the stream, where they lay close in each other's arms. When they knew they must ride on, Jonathan surprised Ann by lifting her onto a pillion cushion on the back of the stallion's saddle. "I want to feel your nearness," he said.

But the little mare whinnied in protest at losing her rider. "Here, Ann, hold her reins and she'll follow."

The handsome stallion turned his head to study the mare. When Big Brown saw that Ginger was not being left behind, he blew a blasting snort through his wide nostrils and took to the trail. The little mare quivered at the sound and promptly trotted into place close behind.

Jonathan spoke of a village called Madison. "Sam Blish has a tavern there, first class for these parts."

"Are you sure there'll be a place for us when taverns are said to be so few?"

"I sent a message by carrier to say I'll be coming and bringing my bride. The taverner and his good wife know me well."

"I've heard tell that often there are many beds in one sleeping room," Ann spoke shyly. "I would not like the sharing."

"This tavern has a Ladies Parlour. I've asked for the placing of a bed there so we may have privacy. There won't be many comforts, Ann, till we get to Washington."

They rode on in silence, each thinking his own thoughts. There was only the sound of their horses hoofs muffled on the woods floor and the evening calls of birds and insects.

Stalwart Big Brown carried them readily through bramble and underbrush, weaving skillfully about the great trees of the forest. Ginger followed confidently. Suddenly the trail came out of the thick groves into a clearing. From the ridge, they caught a view of the waters of the Ohio River, shining broad and beautiful in the twilight.

"I've never seen the Ohio so far from home," Ann spoke eagerly as they pulled up the horses. "No wonder it's called the 'Great River'."

"We're coming close to Madison village. There's smoke rising from a cabin chimney."

"Then I believe it would become me as the wife of a congressman to be seated on my own horse."

"It's fast growing into darkness. There'll be no one about to take note of how we're riding. All right, my shy little wife," as he felt a pleading pressure. "It will be as you wish."

"Always, Mister Jennings?"

"Always, Madame Jennings," and he assisted Ann to remount Ginger.

The trail widened into a dirt road that led through a stretch of log houses. Only an occasional cabin showed the glow of a candle-lantern casting its flickering light. So quiet was the village, the only sounds came from the hoof beats of their own horses pounding on the hard dirt road. "Perhaps everyone will be abed," Ann called fearfully. "We may not be welcomed."

At that moment, Jonathan pointed to a log cabin, looming a little larger than the others.

"Here's our tavern." With a mighty voice, he called out, "Halloo the house! Halloo-o the house!"

Sam Blish came to the door holding his lantern high. "Who's yere? Who's yere? Why if it ain't Congressman Jennings, Sir!"

"Good evening to you, Blish. Here I am with Madame Jennings. I trust my message reached you?"

"I heered, Congressman Jennings, an' ye, Madame, I'm pleased to meetcha." He held his light closer to Ann's face. "Folks been sayin' ez how ye be a mighty purty one and I kin see they wuz tellin' the truth, Ma'am."

Just then, a motherly woman, looking plump from her own good cooking, stepped from the cabin.

"Here's my Missus come to see after ye."

"How-de-do, Madame Jennings, and welcome to ye." Ann nodded, pleased at the sound of her new name. "My, ain't ye the young 'un," the taverner's wife went on, as the men helped Ann dismount. "When was the marryin', Madame Jennings?"

"This very morning, Ma'am. We had to ride off before the celebrating had barely begun."

"Here, boy," from Sam Blish. "See to the horses. The mare acts travel-weary." Then he turned to Jonathan and Ann, "Come in now. We're readied for ye."

They entered the cabin and Ann found herself in a large lantern-lit room. She was surprised to see several men sitting at a table along the wall. She kept her eyes downcast but she sensed that the men were watching as the taverner escorted her across the room.

"Here, Ma'am is the parlour. It's for ladies, only this night ye'll be sharin' with your husband—he hopes," and Sam Blish slapped his thigh with a hearty guffaw.

Ann was startled to hear the men join in the laughter. She blushed and clung to Jonathan's arm.

"See, Congressman Jennings, I moved a bed in like ye asked."

Ann suddenly became aware that their sleeping quarters were in this same room. Mrs. Blish noted Ann's confusion. "See Madame Jennings, here be a curtain to pull. I figured ye'd be wanting to be more to yourselves maybe."

Ann gave her a grateful look.

Sam Blish went on speaking. "There be a looking glass, Madame Jennings, though if ye'll excuse me sayin' so, ye be purty enough not to be needin' no mirror. If'n ye be wantin' food now, the Missus'll bring it."

Again Ann heard snickering from the men across the room and her heart beat as if it would fly from her chest.

"Thank you, Blish," Jonathan spoke. "Leave us a lantern and we'll make ready for tomorrow's journey."

"Good night to ye both then," and Sam Blish and his wife left them alone.

From behind their curtain, Ann could still hear voices and snickerings. Then all at once, there were only sounds of hushed whisperings. The cabin became curiously quiet.

Jonathan peeked through the curtain. "The men are leaving. The tavern's quieting down for the night."

In the light of the lantern, Ann moved to the looking glass. There reflected in the mirror, she was startled to see the flickering lights of many candles. She turned quickly. Outside the one window were shadowy faces pushing and shoving to peer into the room. Ann stood motionless.

"Don't be frightened. Folks are just curious. I'll put out the lantern and the show will be over."

Jonathan doused the light. At the same moment there were violent shouts and cries. In the darkness, Ann tried to run to Jonathan but strong hands grabbed her and pinned her arms to her sides. She tried to scream but no sound came from her tight throat. As she struggled to free herself, a blindfold was knotted roughly across her eyes, and she was lifted, kicking and struggling, and carried into the coolness of the night air.

"Jonathan, Jonathan, where are you?"

A strong hand quickly muffled her mouth. At the same moment she felt herself being pushed into a seat. Whenever she tried to rise, sturdy hands shoved her back. She heard no words but she distinguished the snufflings and clopping hoofs of horses.

Suddenly the strong hands left her mouth and Ann shouted, "Jonathan, Jonathan, I'm being kidnapped. Where are you?"

Then as unexpectedly as she had been seized, rough fingers were untying the hard knots of her blindfold. In the darkness of the night, Ann still could see nothing. Then someone raised a lantern and she saw her husband. He was seated on a stool on the opposite end of the wagon where they had taken her. He too was blindfolded but his hands were free and he was working desperately to pull the binding knots apart.

Ann cried out to him when suddenly the wagon was surrounded on all sides. Shouting villagers held lanterns high.

"Surprise, surprise! It's a shivaree! A shivaree! A warming for the bride and groom."

Pandemonium broke out as all the village gathered about the wagon. Folks sang and shouted and banged pots and kettles. They whistled and cheered the newly-married couple.

Free of his blindfold at last, Jonathan tried to make Ann hear over the noise. "Don't be afraid. It's their way of congratulating us."

A team stood hitched to the wagon and suddenly the driver clucked the horses. The wagon took off so abruptly Ann fell backwards off the wagon seat where strange hands had carried her, and Jonathan moved beside her. Shouting and singing, the crowd ran after the wagon as the horses galloped off.

Up and down the short village street, the wagon carried the couple until at last it stopped once more at the Blish Tavern. Once again, Ann was surprised for there a great feast had been laid. Lanterns cast their wavering lights on platters of wild turkey and smoked pork. There was fresh-churned butter and preserves for the johnny-cakes. Great kegs of apple cider and more spiritous liquids waited to quench thirsty throats.

"Come, Madame Jennings," called Jonathan, "try the pumpkin preserves on the cornbread." But Ann was still trembling from the shock.

"Ready for a hoe-down, Madame Jennings?" called Sam Blish, scraping on his fiddle while the blacksmith blew on a whistle as folks were matching partners. "Everyone'll be wantin' to dance with the purtiest bride in the whole Indiana Territory."

Ann stood bewildered and hung back at the side of her husband.

"Come, Ann, this is a celebrating party for our marriage," Jonathan whispered to her. "It should make up for the one we had to leave behind."

"Ye see, Madame Jennings," added Blish, "that husband of yours—he's like one of us. None of that actin' the aristycrat like ol' William Henry Harrison."

The blacksmith added his praise. "Madame, I've seen Congressman Jennings roll logs right along side o' us and carry up a corner all the while he's talkin' things like taxes and how we oughter vote fer him."

Still others spoke up. "Yep, folks kin trust the likes o' Jennings a representin' us. One of these days I reckon he'll be gittin' Indiana fer a state."

"Yeah, and a road for tradin' like those Eastern folks got."

"He's a jovial drinker, too, like the rest of us," and the men escorted Jonathan to join the jollification.

"Why, these are friends to my Jonathan," Ann was thinking. "This is their way of honoring him." And she let herself be coaxed into the merrymaking. Soon she was dancing the do-si-doe's as light as if she hadn't travelled all day in the saddle.

Hours flew by until the party grew rowdy and bid to go on all night. Jonathan pulled Ann aside. "You've had your wedding festivities after all, little Ann. Let's be sneaking away now. Folks are so busy with the celebrating, we shan't be missed."

"O Jonathan, I can't bear to have our wedding day come to an end."

"Maybe it's like Becky said—'it's just a wondrous beginning day'."

So they stole back to the Ladies Parlour in the one-room tavern. In the early dawn Ann and Jonathan were ready to resume their journey. They found the tavern floor covered with sprawling bodies sleeping off last night's merrymaking. Ann giggled when she saw them but Jonathan put his fingers to his lips and they tiptoed carefully over the snoring slumberers.

They found their horses groomed and saddled and Sam Blish waiting with his wife to bid them Godspeed.

"We took the liberty, Ma'am, of makin' a food packet for your journey. There be johnny-cake and cold beans with clover honey for the sweetenin'," Sam's wife spoke.

"I'll be remembering your kindly hospitality, Madame Blish. I hope Congressman Jennings will bring me this way again."

"Ye'd best come with him all right," Sam spoke. "Folks'll be wantin' him for governor when statehood comes and he's picked hisself a winnin' vote-getter to marry up with." Ann blushed as she curtsied at the compliment.

"A road safe for travelling and trading is what we need for statehood. But I see the River's glistening already with sun-up. Many thanks, my friends," and he mounted Big Brown while the taverner helped Ann to her saddle from the upping block.

As graceful Ginger danced smartly beside the stallion Sam Blish asked, "Do ye reckon your mare can take the rough ridin' ye'll be meetin', Madame Jennings? Ye be headin' her for mighty wild country, Ma'am."

Before Ann could reply, Big Brown had plunged forward and Ginger took after him. But Sam Blish's Missus answered.

"I be reckonin' on *both* the lady and the mare—they got spunk, those two."

The short village street came to an abrupt end and once more the riders found themselves swallowed up in dense growth of trees and brush.

"This is an old buffalo trail," said Jonathan, "made years ago by buffalo tromping a path to some salt lick."

The horses now must crash through thick underbrush. Big Brown often turned his head with a flick of his ears as if to encourage Ginger following close behind.

As the riders left the high river bank, travel turned truly grim. After many tedious hours, the forest gave signs of thinning. "I see a clearing ahead at last," Jonathan called back to Ann, still struggling against branches that clawed her hair and smacked against her face.

At that moment savage yells broke through the quiet. Big Brown reared and plunged but Jonathan managed to keep his seat. Ginger stopped so abruptly that Ann was left dangling from her saddle's pommel. She made no outcry but fought desperately to keep a grip on the quivering mare.

Across the clearing, two men rose from behind a fallen log, and came running toward them yelling wildly and aiming rifles. Then they halted as suddenly as they had appeared.

"Mon Dieu, it is Congressman Jennings!"

Jonathan dismounted as both men put down their rifles.

"A thousand apologies, Monsieur Jennings! We figured you be rivermen," spoke one with a French accent.

"We make apology for our rude welcome, M'sieur, but we don't often see travellers and we have need to protect our vineyards."

"Oui, M'sieur, rivermen are a bad lot and they often head through here returning north to pick up another river job. We have need to take care."

15

"It is well, Gentlemen. This should make me more alert on the trail. It is my first time to travel with a lady. I ride with my bride, Gentlemen." Then turning to Ann, "These are the brothers Dufours—John and James."

Ann's knees were still shaking but Jonathan helped her to dismount and she managed a curtsy to the men who bowed gallantly.

"And such a pretty one, if you please, Madame. Your husband helped us roll the logs for our cabins, Madame Jennings. May we invite you to stay the night? We make much celebration for the bride with music and dancing and much good wine from our vineyards."

Ann whispered to Jonathan, "Not another shivaree tonight, please Jonathan."

"Good folk, we thank you but we have need to travel more miles before sunset."

"Stay a little then."

So the Jennings allowed themselves to be escorted through fertile acres where blue clusters of Madeira grapes hung heavy on the vines.

"We make 2000 gallons of wines now. We plant eight acres, Monsieur." John pointed proudly to the lush fruit.

"Plenty families come now," added John as they saw men, women, and children at work in the vineyards. "Beaucoup votes for you, eh Monsieur?" and they all laughed.

Faces were cheerful under their pretty straw sun hats as they came forward to welcome the travellers. Soon they were bringing their guests baskets of wine and cheese and breads of rare white flours. They toasted the bride and groom again and again in French and a little in English.

When the guests had to leave, the children crowded about Ginger, curious about the strange sidesaddle where a lady sat with her legs both on the same side of the horse with a pommel for her knee.

Ann communicated with gestures and when she admired the women's pretty straw sun hats they showed her the special knot used to hold the strips together without sewing.

"Voila—le chapeau!" said one.

"Le chapeau? Bonnet?" inquired Ann.

"Oui, oui!" The women were delighted to hear Ann say their French word.

16

They pointed to Ginger—"un cheval."

"A horse—un cheval? Merci—thank you?" Ann repeated.

"Je vous aime—I love you," Ann slowly imitated.

The children giggled at a grown-up trying to say what was so easy for them. One little girl stepped forward holding her own pretty straw hat out to Ann. "Je vous aime. J'ai envie de vous donner mon petit chapeau, s'il vous plait."

Ann could not understand the words but she recognized that this was a gift. She kissed the little girl and then fastened the pretty hat on her head tying it securely under her chin. The women oohed and ahed in delight and when Ann spoke their word "Merci", the children clapped their hands. At the excitement, Ginger began to whinny and shake her head up and down.

"My mare is jealous of my chapeau," laughed Ann.

One of the women fitted a partly-finished bonnet over Ginger's ears. "Pour un cheval!" Then there was more laughter and chattering and gesturing.

"Truly, Monsieur Dufours, we have gained more friendships than votes, but I will be seeking a road for transporting your delicious wines, you may be sure."

As usual, Big Brown was impatient to be off. As they rode from the clearing, Ann tried to get her husband's attention. "Is my new chapeau not becoming?" she persisted coyly.

But Jonathan was not listening. He was gazing back at the lush lands they were leaving. "If only we can get an east-west road across the country, more emigrants like the Dufours' families will help build a great state for Indiana."

Ann sighed. She was learning that even on a honeymoon, a bride cannot expect all of her husband's attention.

The trail led them now along a high ridge overlooking La Belle Riviere as their French friends called the beautiful Ohio. They came to a stand of majestic beech trees, so wide that not even Jonathan could reach his arms around one. The horses picked their way through the dense growths of black walnut trees and honey locusts, heavy with wild grapes. For the first time, Ann heard the shrill screams of the paroquet and caught the flash of its beautiful red, green, and yellow colors.

They came finally into a deep descent that took them into narrow bottom lands where vegetation grazed their sides. Ginger was almost hidden in the tall vegetation as they splashed through the mucky swamp.

On reaching higher ground at last they dismounted to rest when Ann let out a shriek. "Oh, my beautiful skirt! It's coated with mud," and she wrung her hands in despair.

"Good heavens, Ann, you were brave enough before the Dufours' rifles—yet here you carry on over a muddied skirt."

This time it was Ann who was not listening, as she tried to scrape away the clinging scum of the stagnant water from her new riding skirt. It was Jonathan's turn to sigh, "I have much to understand about a lady—especially my own."

The trail began to climb again. Now the horses must pull up steep slopes cut by deep ravines until they reached a plateau where their riders could see land cleared for cabins that clustered among the standing trees.

"We've come to a settlement of Quaker Friends."

"Are we to be greeted again with rifles?"

"Quakers do not believe in violence. I know these Friends—Enoch and Abigail Evens were neighbors to my family back in Pennsylvania."

Already the sound of the horses had alerted the tiny settlement and men, women, and children came running to greet the arrival of visitors so rare in these parts.

The men wore black flat-brimmed hats set square on their heads. The women were plainly dressed in grey homespun with caps held fast over simple hair-do's. Some wore bonnets over the close-fitting caps and shoulder shawls against the chill of early evening. Little girls were dressed like exact copies of their mothers.

Enoch and Abigail stepped forward to welcome them as the riders dismounted. "God's greeting to thee, Jonathan. 'Tis good to see thee again." Then turning to Ann, "and thou must be one we've heard spoken of with high praise." Abigail took Ann's tiny hands into her own and kissed her on the forehead, "Jonathan's wife is truly welcome."

"Thy husband helped us raise the roof-tree of our cabin," Enoch spoke. "It is fitting that thou should stay the night within."

Others came forward now. "We are birthright Quakers here. Sister Abigail is our minister," said one.

"A woman minister?" Ann failed to hold back her surprise.

"In the Society of Friends, women have the same rights as men have," the Quaker explained.

Abigail spoke up then. "Enough of Quaker rights while our guests must be hungry for their supper. Will thee come with me, Madame Jennings?"

"You show us great kindness," and she followed Abigail to the cabin.

Enoch began to help Jonathan with the horses. "I've never seen a horse like this one," as he stroked the little mare.

"My wife is devoted to this horse—who doesn't always wear a hat." He laughed as he curried the finely molded head and powerful shoulders.

"How's she managing the rough terrain?"

"She's small but she shows tremendous power in her muscles. We're told that her father is a great weight-puller. She is thought to be a descendant of the horse of Justin Morgan of probable Thoroughbred and Arabian lineage."

"Dost thou truly mean to ride thy young wife through the wilderness all the way to the East on this horse?"

Jonathan's face grew solemn. "If God be willing. Both Madame Jennings and the mare show stamina and courage."

"Thy wife must indeed be a brave woman." The two horses whinnied almost in harmony as Enoch stabled them in a three-sided lean-to. "Until our cabin was built, this lean-to was our only shelter that first spring. Like thy wife, my Abigail also has spirit and courage."

Abigail had led Ann to a cabin almost hidden in the thick grove of trees. Flat stones made a walk where marigolds stood bright in a spot of sunlight freed from tree shade. The cabin held one window where in place of precious glass, the pages of letters had been pasted into the window frame. The paper had been greased to make it translucent. Ann was surprised to recognize Jonathan's handwriting on the letter pages.

"Thy husband's letters truly enlighten us as he keeps us informed." Both women laughed as they made ready to enter the cabin.

Abigail lifted the latchstring hanging on the outside of the split-timbered door to raise the heavy bar inside. As the door opened, they were almost engulfed by children of all ages and sizes.

"Ezekial here is the eldest," as Abigail presented each of her children.

"Here is Rachel and Isaac and Priscilla and Sarah and Samuel." Each girl curtsied to Ann and the boys bowed.

"Obadiah and Jehu are in the garden," as she continued. "And this is our newest—Baby Elvira," taking a plump baby from the wooden cradle. "Now sit thee down by the fire then and rest from thy travel while preparations go forth for thy supper."

"You seem to be well situated, Madame Evens. How long have you lived here?"

"We've not lived the year's full seasons yet and the men had first to clear land for planting corn and potatoes. Soon we'll be hearing the ring of the axe as they begin to girdle more trees to shut off the sap. When the leaves die down come winter, the trees will be ready to cut down to make more cleared land. My husband has even promised me space for a garden for herbs so I won't have to be searching the woods."

"Herbs for cures? My little brothers pretend to a fit of hiccups just to taste the dill."

Abigail laughed. "I'll be planting seeds in the spring. Seed-swapping is mighty important hereabouts."

"When my husband comes this way again, might he not bring you seeds for the planting?"

"I declare, a gift of seeds would get thy Jonathan a vote for every seed, especially if women could vote."

"Ladies vote?"

Abigail laughed. "Thee must know nothing is impossible when I witness thee, wife to a congressman journeying across the country to Washington City and on horseback. Thou art truly a brave one."

All this time, Abigail had given quiet orders to each of the children. Rachel stirred the squirrel meat stewing in the pot that hung from the wooden trammel high in the stick-and-clay chimney. Priscilla mixed corn dodgers to bake in a long-handled skillet over the log-heap fire. With a gourd, Sarah ladled water into a three-legged spider-pan to boil the cabbage that Isaac brought from the garden.

Obadiah had carried water from the spring and Ezekial dug sweet potatoes to bake in the ashes of the fire. Even the smallest children helped. They placed the pewter plates and spoons, and cups of tin about the long pine table standing in the middle of the

20

cabin. But two blue-edged china plates meant for the special guests, Abigail herself took care to handle.

Finally slab benches and three-legged puncheon stools were pulled up to the table. Great logs on the hearth gave warmth against the chill from the nearby forests and the firelight illumined the room. Yet Abigail lit one tallow candle for the table.

"To use this candle be an extravagance," Ann heard Abigail speak low to Rachel, "but it's not often we can extend hospitality to a congressman and his bride."

"Nor any guests at all—ever!" Ann heard the young daughter sigh wistfully.

The men entered and all quickly took places at the table and bowed their heads. Enoch said the blessing: "Help us, O God, to follow the Divine Spark that is in each of us. Teach us to listen to Thy voice within our hearts and to quake and tremble at Thy name. Help us to do Thy will as Thou commands. *A-men!*"

"Amen!"

The children were quick to burst into chatter, full of questions for their guests. "Why dost thy horse wear a hat? Why dost thou ride a saddle on its side instead of astride like a man? Dost thou have a baby? Why not?"

Enoch spoke finally. "Curb thy tongues, children. Let the grown-ups speak now. Jonathan, dost thou bring us word of Indiana's statehood?"

"The quota needed must be near 60,000 but the population of the whole Territory is still only at 5,000. Emigration would come fast if we could convince Congress how much a national road is needed. I mean to try when I reach Washington City."

"It is true the settlers have much need for a road. Our women never complain but they lack much to make their lives tolerable—like education for the children, freedom from the sicknesses—so many needs."

While the men talked politics, Ann listened with great interest. When the older children had put the little ones to bed in the loft above, they were permitted, for such a special occasion, to take a few early-harvested ears of popcorn from the drying. They threw the dried grains into the embers, and then scrambled to catch the exploded kernels that popped snow-white in all directions. There was much laughter as Ann, too, learned to catch the fluffy kernels.

"Come children, thee will wear out thy guest. Madame Jennings has had a day of much journey and a far way yet to travel."

So now the fire was banked for morning and the children climbed the ladder to the loft. What was left of the company candle had long since been extinguished to be saved for another occasion. Enoch pulled in the latchstring so no one outside could lift the great bar that held the door closed. Jonathan and Ann were given a bed standing in a corner where posts fastened to floor and rafters held poles to support the frame for a feather mattress.

Jonathan fell asleep immediately but Ann lay awake. She could hear the bull frogs—"jug-o'-rum, jug-o'-rum" they seemed to call. She heard the rustle of cornhusk mattresses in the loft overhead as the children turned in their sleeping. From across the cabin came the sounds of Abigail tending the baby in the trundle bed.

Ann knew that tomorrow they would be riding out of the Indiana Territory where Congressman Jennings was known and welcomed. The trail would lead into the wilderness of Ohio with more ancient tall trees, with malarial waters, Indian camps and wild animals. Even in this cabin of good will, a flintlock rifle was lodged over the door in the forked branch of a dogwood tree.

Ann tossed sleeplessly. "Will I be equal to the hazards that lie ahead" she worried, "and will my mare?"

Suddenly Jonathan in his sleep flung his arm protectively about her. Ann slept then, secure in the comfort of her husband's love.

III
A Night In The Forest

First Day started early in the Quaker cabin. The guests were escorted to the Quaker Meeting House, built first before all the cabins. On crude benches that lined the clay-chinked walls, the Quaker Friends were in their places. Men sat on one side and women and children on the other.

"Quakers believe," Abigail had said, "that God is in everyone and can be heard through a still small voice within us, if only we will listen." The Friends were listening.

After a period of silence, Abigail rose and spoke in gentle voice. "The power of goodness in each of us is stronger than the power of evil. Help us, O Lord, to hear the inner voice Thou uses to guide us."

The Meeting was at a close, and the Friends gathered about the Jennings to wish them Godspeed. Enoch took Ann aside.

"We have known thy husband as a boy growing up in the love of his family. Jonathan holds against slavery." Then his face grew stern. "Thou grew up in Kentucky—a state that holds with slavery. What stand dost thou take?"

Ann was taken back. No one had ever asked her such a question before. Many of her Kentucky friends owned slaves and their own Becky had come with the family when they moved from George Town. Before Ann could reply, Abigail came to her.

"I'm taking the liberty of seeking thy delivery of a letter to my close friend Dolley Madison. She is a birthright Quaker and we were friends in Virginia before she became the wife of the President of the United States."

"You mean I'll be carrying a letter to the wife of the President?" Ann tucked the letter securely in her saddle pouch.

"I understand that being the President's wife has not changed Dolley's true kindness," Abigail answered.

Ginger nuzzled Ann for attention now and Big Brown pawed the earth with his usual impatience. Reluctantly, the Jennings left their friends and once more rode from the sunlight into the ever-present twilight of the forest.

The horses twisted and veered through endless trees until several hours later, Jonathan suddenly pulled up on Big Brown.

Barely distinguishable in the rough underbrush were two branching footways.

"Here we must choose trails. If we take this road along the river, several days will be added to our journey."

"Would that make us late for the opening of the Congress?"

"Yes, especially if Congress convenes early. There is much agitation over the British forcing our American seamen into service on their ships."

"Then we should take the shorter road and arrive on time."

"The shorter road would also make it possible to visit my family in Pennsylvania. I have already posted a letter by carrier that I hoped to bring them the fairest bride in the land."

"O Jonathan—I am shy to meet your family. They are all so educated—ministers, and doctors and all. Will they think me a fit wife for such an important son?"

"Nonsense, Ann," taking her into his arms, "but you'd best know this shorter trail holds the more perils."

Ann drew back. She studied Jonathan's face. Was he thinking of Indian camps? Or of the wild animals of the ancient forests? Or was he concerned for the fevers of the seasons?

"We shall be finding fewer overnight cabins spaced farther apart, Ann. Would you be afraid to sleep in the woods?"

"Is that all? It's more frightening to be meeting my new kinfolk. What of you, Ginger?" stroking the mare. "Shall we follow wherever they lead us?" Ginger tossed her head and nickered.

"It's agreed then. We'll take the shorter trail." But Ann noticed how carefully Jonathan made sure that his rifle lay ready before him across his saddle.

He led the way now through mile after mile of gigantic trees closing them in like walls. The horses tunneled through tangles of vines to follow a barely discernible trail.

"Shawnee Indians made this trail years ago moving from their council fire to hunting grounds."

"Are there Indians in these forests now?"

Jonathan only laughed at Ann's concern. "When so many settlers took their lands, the Indians had to find new hunting grounds. They hunt far north now."

But the trunks of the great trees were so wide that an Indian could run from one to another to ambush an unsuspecting enemy.

And moccasined feet could move silently in the muck of fallen leaves that covered the forest floor.

Jonathan kept his rifle ready.

Already there were signs of autumn. Nuts dropped from hickory trees, as squirrels raced from one branch to another scolding at the sound of hoof beats breaking into the forest stillness.

Tree branches slapped against Ann and the sharp-edged bushes crowded close. "Shawnee Indians must not have used horses on this trail—it's not even wide enough for Ginger."

"Shawnee are walking people. They half-run single file. Each Indian steps into the footprints of the one ahead."

"What if a short Indian follows a tall one?"

Jonathan laughed. "All Shawnee are tall." Just then, he pulled Big Brown up abruptly. "Whoa! Whoa there!"

A great mud hole stretched wide before them, yawning like a deep crater. "It's a buffalo hole. The trail is blocked."

"Buffalos?—O where?"

"They're gone—years ago. Early Indians hunted them out. They must have used this trail on the way to some salt lick."

Ann pulled Ginger up closer. "However did they make such a mud hole. Isn't it too deep for Ginger? Please don't make us cross through, Jonathan—I'll get more mud on my skirt."

"It's too deep to cross on the horses, all right. Buffalos must have rolled over and over in the mud to coat their hides from gnats and flies." Jonathan dismounted.

"Where are you going? Don't leave—it's spooky here."

"I'm looking for a crossing. Here—here's a tree big enough to serve. It must have been felled by lightning. It's broad enough that we can balance on foot, but the horses will have to walk the bog."

Jonathan and Ann stepped slowly and carefully across the rough trunk, but the horses were in trouble. Big Brown plowed through the sticky mud that sucked at his legs like molasses on a stirring stick. Ginger made little whimpering sounds as she tried to follow the stallion. Her feet slipped often and kept sinking deep over her fetlocks till the mud splattered even her belly.

"Poor Ginger, she's so frightened. Can't you help her, Jonathan?" But he could only call out "Steady, steady, Girl."

Like quicksand, the bog pulled on the mare's slender legs

25

until finally she stood mud-covered and dejected at the side of Big Brown, safely past the buffalo hole.

"Don't fret. A good plunge in a stream will wash the mud off the horses."

They walked the horses then seeking water, but when they finally came to a stream, early fall rains had swollen it into a river. It was too deep and wide to be ridden across.

"You rest, Ann, while I search for some crossing."

The horses were trying to shake off their mud clobbers when Jonathan called out. "Come see, here's an abandoned raft."

There, almost hidden by overhanging branches, was a small raft tied fast to a willow tree. It was just a few logs tied together with heavy vines and could scarcely hold two passengers and their gear.

"Could it be an Indian raft? O Jonathan!"

But Jonathan ignored the question. "The horses will have to swim. Has the mare ever been in deep water?"

"Indeed not! She would surely drown."

"Then I guess we'll have to leave her behind," Jonathan spoke matter-of-factly. Without further words, he set about removing the saddles from the two horses and stowing them on the small raft with the rest of their gear. "I can pole us across. Come aboard now."

"I'll not be stepping on that raft and leave Ginger behind. We'll wait till the water goes down." Ann sat down obstinately on a nearby boulder. Ginger followed her, nuzzling gently on her arm, but in her anger, Ann pushed the mare away.

Big Brown now free of his saddle moved toward the stream. First he shook off the great clobbers of mud. Then he plunged deep into the waters where his feet no longer touched the rocky bottom of the stream. Only his great head and ears showed as he began to swim toward the farther shore.

Used to following Big Brown's every lead, Ginger trotted to the water but there the little horse stopped. She whinnied piteously but seeing Big Brown leaving her behind, she stepped skittishly into the swollen stream. It was too deep for the small mare. She lost her footing and the cold water closed over her head.

"O Jonathan, she's drowning, she's drowning. My beautiful mare! O save her, do something!"

Scarcely realizing what was happening, Ann let herself be coaxed on to the raft. Jonathan began to pole it across the water following the swimming animals.

Big Brown reached the embankment where he reared and crashed about the underbrush neighing triumphantly as if to encourage Ginger. The spunky little mare flounced and floundered, trying to keep her head above the waters until at last her feet once more touched solid ground.

Barely waiting for the raft to touch the shore, Ann jumped off and rushed to Ginger as the mare shook off the last of the mud clobbers. The little mare began to swish her tail from side to side to drive the water-flies from her wet rumps. She held her head once more as if proud of her achievement.

Ann was angry with Jonathan. "Why did you do this to my mare? She might have drowned. What a terrible danger!"

Jonathan spoke no words but proceeded to unload the makeshift raft and tend to the horses. The mare stood quietly while he groomed her dry. Big Brown nudged at the little mare but Ginger danced nimbly away as if she, too, were angry.

Jonathan talked to Big Brown as he curried the great horse but his words were meant for Ann's ears. "Ginger's gentleness covers a horse as wiry as steel," he spoke. "The mare can climb hills and leap logs and now we know she can swim in deep water. She's a fine-spirited mare to be trusted to carry our mistress the hard ways to Washington City."

Ann heard but she remained aloof.

"It's difficult understanding a wife," Jonathan sighed.

They had travelled far that day and were still a long way from a tavern or a friendly cabin. "I think it best if we stay the night here beside the stream. A good rest may restore cheerful relations." Jonathan spoke to Ann this time, but she made no reply.

Jonathan went to work moving the saddles and bags to a dry place to make camp for the night. He left the horses untied, free to seek swampy pasture by the stream. Big Brown found the water-grass not to his liking and began to nibble on the trunk of a tree tearing off small flakes of bark which he chewed with obvious satisfaction. At first, Ginger paid no attention. She had never eaten bark from a tree but now she followed Big Brown's every move. Soon both horses were munching bark from the same tree.

27

Ann still sat withdrawn. In the fast-darkening woods, she was filled with great loneliness and homesickness. She was less angry now, but she pretended disinterest as Jonathan prepared for their night in the forest.

Twilight comes early to the tree-world so Jonathan hastened to cast a fishing line into a pool made by the stream. Soon he had caught a fish big enough for their supper. Ann stole admiring glances at his deft movements in preparing the fish. Finally, her curiosity got the better of her irritation.

"What kind of fish have you caught, Mister Jennings?"

"It's a catfish, Madame Jennings. They're plentiful here."

"What be you doing with that metal box?"

"This is a tinder box. It holds dry punk for starting a fire. See!"

He applied the spark from the flint to a small pile of dry twigs and a bright flame began to show. Taking an iron spider skillet from his saddlebag and a bit of salt and pork grease, he soon had the fish sizzling. From their provisions, he produced corn meal then.

"What be you doing now, my Jonathan?"

"Did I hear you say *my* Jonathan?" He stopped his preparations and looked longingly at Ann. The light from the fire was on her face and Jonathan thought she had never looked so lovely. "Does that mean I am forgiven for whatever it was that estranged you?"

Ann rose impulsively from her log seat and suddenly she was enfolded in Jonathan's arms. Reconciliation was complete.

"The fish is burning!"

When order was restored, Jonathan showed Ann how to make johnny-cakes from the cornmeal. They mixed it with clear water from the stream and shaped cakes to bake on a clapboard of green wood that Jonathan tilted against the hot ashes of the fire. He taught her to flip the cake up in the air and then catch it back on the board. Ann's first cake missed the board and fell into the ashes. As their laughter filtered through the woods, the two horses flicked their ears and went on chomping together.

Jonathan was loud in praise of his wife's first johnny-cakes, tender and appetizing under their sweetening of honey. At home, Becky had reigned over the family kitchen and she considered cooking unladylike for a young belle like Ann.

"How surprised Becky would be to see me, wife to a congressman, cooking over a campfire in the wilderness!"

Before the twilight deepened finally into blackness, Jonathan hastened to prepare for their sleeping. First, he hobbled the horses with ligaments of bark to keep them from straying into the woods. Then he shaped their saddle blankets into a small tent setting it over boughs of sassafrass, spread to make the earth soft for their bed.

Stars peeked through the branches of the trees and fireflies glowed like candle-lanterns. Suddenly from the black shadows of the forest, came a long tremulous cry shattering the stillness of the night.

"Hoo-hoo-O-hoo-hooo-o!"

Ann clung to Jonathan.

"It's only the hooting of an owl." Then the eerie notes came again.

"Hoo-hoo-O-hoo-hooo-o!"

Ann clung more tightly. "I've heard tell that Indians imitate such calls for signals. Stay close to me, Jonathan, I'm fearful."

"Fearful of an owl protecting baby owlets? But I'll keep the fire high beside us. If there be no animals to devour us, mosquitos will."

They lay together then in their blanket tent in the profound silence of the forest. Even the owl had quieted. The only sounds came from evening breezes whispering through tall branches high above them like a soft-sung lullaby.

Ann fell quickly asleep in the security of her husband's arms but Jonathan lay awake, listening, with rifle close. He heard a rustling sound from the underbrush and listened to the restless movements of the two horses. Careful not to disturb the sleeping Ann, Jonathan crept from the tent. With rifle pointing into the darkness, he threw a bit of brimstone on the fire to strengthen the flame. Standing so that he would not be silhouetted by its light, he listened intently. The strange rustling had ceased, and he could distinguish no moving shadows. All was quiet.

Jonathan trusted the horses' instinct for danger. When they seemed to settle down to chomping, he moved back into the tent and quickly fell into exhausted sleep.

Both awakened at the first sifting of sunlight through the trees. The songs of early birds were filling the fresh air of dawn when they heard a male voice singing.

"That's no owl. Is it an Indian?" whispered Ann.

The voice came louder and nearer:

"Oh, the red, rosy apple,
The round tasty apple
That grows on the old apple tree.
With each juicy bite
Toast the apple tonight;
Oh, the red, rosy apple for me."*

"Why, that's Johnny Appleseed's song!" Jonathan spoke.

"Who keeps the house?" came a voice close by. "Anybody within?" and Jonathan was fast out of the tent.

Ann watched him throw his arms about a strange barefoot man with a deerhide pack on his back. His trousers were old and his shirt looked like a coffee sack turned upside down with holes to let his head through. He wore an iron cooking pot on his head like a hat. In his hand, instead of a rifle, he carried a book.

When Ann appeared, the little man spoke, "A good morrow to you, Ma'am." He took off his mush-pan hat and held it out. "I come to barter for my breakfast, Ma'am. If your johnny-cakes be appetizing, I kin offer some fresh fall applesass to make them more so."

"A good morrow to you, Mister Appleseed, Sir." Ann curtsied.

Both men laughed. "My name is John Chapman but folks call me Johnny Appleseed 'cause I go about giving apple seeds to any who will clear land for the planting of an orchard."

Ann blushed at her mistake.

"You see, Ma'am, apple seeds make an easy start for a needed pioneerin' crop. 'Sides, nothin' smells better cookin' or eatin' than a kettle o' apple butter."

"Or the sweet taste of sparkling applejack," added Jonathan smacking his lips.

---

* Permission of Newell H. Long from *Corydon, Cradle of Our Commonwealth,* Sesquicentennial Pageant for first capital of Indiana, 1966, by Eleanor and Newell Long.

"So here's to the rosy red apple, with each juicy bite. . ." the little man began to sing again as he offered tasty pippins from his knapsack. Soon they were all singing as they hastened to prepare their breakfast.

THE RED, ROSY APPLE

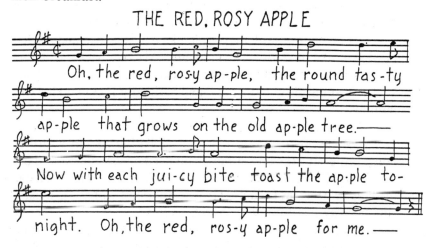

Oh, the red, rosy ap-ple, the round tas-ty ap-ple that grows on the old ap-ple tree.——
Now with each jui-cy bite toast the ap-ple to-night. Oh, the red, ros-y ap-ple for me.——

"Ann heard an owl last night. She needs reassuring that it was not an Indian signal."

"It was an owl all right, but I was the trespasser. When I saw your fire, I came close but I had the shakin' ager so bad I feared to disturb you. I spent the night in an old buckeye tree."

"You slept in a tree?" Ann was amazed.

"Yep, I get nearer heaven thataway. But last night I had the shakin' so bad that my sleepin' tree vibrated like a fiddle string. I had to tie myself to the branches so I wouldn't shake out."

"O Mister Chapman, Sir, you are ill. I could make you sassafrass tea?"

"I thank you, Ma'am but 'twas only the ever-other-day ager. The fever and chills have passed now till the next time. 'Sides it ain't the right season to be drinkin' tea of the sassafrass. Drinkin' it in the autumn ud thin my blood, so come winter, I'd be certain to freeze to death."

"Then could I prepare you tea from the wild cherry like Mama taught me."

"Does it taste bad? Indian medicine man say, 'no hurt, no cure'," and he laughed.

"You are friend to Indians?"

"Indians accept me. They call me the 'orchard god'. I never do them harm and they think I'm brave for they've seen me walk the wilderness like them."

"You have no horse?" Ann asked anxiously. "And if I may speak of it, no boots for the sharpness of the path?"

"I come from walkin' people like the Shawnee and my feet have skin like the hide of an elephant. My feet have carried me through snow and swamps—even thickets where if I stepped on a snake, it would die o' bitin' me," and his kindly eyes twinkled with humour.

"Poisonous snakes!" Ann shuddered.

"Well, Ma'am, rattlesnakes give folks fair warnin' with their noisy rattle. It's the copperhead you need be watchin' for. They sneak out of the canebrakes in silence 'n their fanged jaws kin dart forth as swift as an Indian's arrow. But don't worry—a snake'll slither away fast from your horses' hoofs."

Jonathan hastened to change the subject. "You're carrying apple seeds to new country? Do you think you could carry seeds to our Quaker Friends in Indiana?"

Just then, they heard Big Brown and Ginger nickering for attention. Johnny Appleseed gave each of the horses a sheep-nosed apple.

"Was it you who quieted the horses last night?" asked Jonathan. Johnny nodded.

"I come from the cider presses of Pennsylvania. I can bring you greeting from your father."

"From my father?" Jonathan spoke in surprise.

"Many's the night the Reverend Jennings and I have spent by the same fire when we'd meet in the shades of the forest. He'd be ridin' his preachin' circuit, carryin' the word of the Testament and I'd be carryin' my apple seeds."

"We're on the trail to visit him on our way to Washington City. Do you have fresh news of Tecumseh? Is it true he is organizing the Indian tribes into a confederacy?"

"Would you not rather seek fresh news from Heaven?" Not waiting for an answer, he produced the book Ann had seen him carrying. It was a well-worn Bible and Johnny Appleseed began to read aloud.

"Who can find a virtuous woman, for her price is far above rubies... She will do him good and not evil all the days of her life... She openeth her mouth with wisdom; and in her tongue is the law of kindness."

He proceeded then to tear out the pages he had just read and extend them to Ann. "I give you these words of God's blessings for your marriage."

A spiritual light seemed to shine on the kindly face of this singular little man. Ann was deeply touched as she accepted the gift and she curtsied low.

Then as unexpectedly as he had appeared, Johnny Appleseed made ready to leave. Drawing a wild turkey feather from his knapsack, he fastened it in his hair. About his neck, he hung his mush pot and began to beat it in rhythm. Then waving farewell, he marched briskly forward into the forest singing to the beat of his drum:

"A Yankee boy is trim and tall
And never over fat, Sir
At dance or frolic, hop, and ball
As nimble as a rat, Sir.
Yankee doodle, doodle, do
Yankee doodle dandy. . . . . ."

There was no looking back. The beat of Johnny Appleseed's mush-pan drum and his marching song continued to sound through the woods, growing gradually fainter and fainter. The forest suddenly seemed empty without the warm presence of their extraordinary friend.

Ann carefully tucked away the precious apple seeds he had given her to carry to Dolley Madison. "Maybe one day we could be eating apples from these very seeds in Washington City."

"That depends on how many terms I am elected to the Congress."

"Will I be a help to your elections?"

"It's like Sam Blish said—I married a charming vote-getter."

"But couldn't I do more—I'm learning about our country."

"How could you help? Ladies can't vote."

"Who knows—like Abigail said—maybe some day!"

"Like a hundred years from now?" Jonathan laughed. Then he saw how serious Ann looked and he hastened to add, "The next time I go out into the Territory for the vote, I'll take you along now that I have seen what a good traveller you are proving to be." Then he couldn't resist, "Can you roll logs or carry up a corner?"

"Now Jonathan, don't be teasing. While you talk with the men, I could visit with the women to learn of their needs. I can rock babies and help where there's sickness." Then she added triumphantly, "And I can carry seeds."

They rode side-by-side now on a wider trail. "Jonathan, why are you against slavery?"

"Indeed, I believe no one should be possessed by another."

"Then what about our Becky and her boy? Are they not slaves?"

"Your father didn't believe in slavery either. He gave Becky manumission papers that set them free when he carried them to Indiana from Kentucky."

"But they stayed on with us? She's like family. Did she ask Papa for her freedom?"

"Most likely she wanted it for her boy. She worried that he might not be so fortunate to serve in a family like yours."

Ann was quiet, thinking of the question Enoch Evens had asked her. Perhaps she was listening for her answer from an inner voice like the Quakers.

Once again the trail narrowed. It led them away from the stream and the sunlight. They rode now through miles of the tallest tulip trees in the world. Wild hogs feeding on acorns fallen from ancient oaks scattered awkwardly from the horses' hoofs.

Ginger reared in astonishment once as a possum lumbered clumsily from her hoofs. At the sound of the horses, a deer with her tiny fawn beside her, froze in the camouflage of wild pea vines.

The horses were in fine fettle for the day's travel. Although both preferred a good gallop across an open field with the wind in their ears, they stepped carefully through the undergrowth of the trail. On the steep ascents, Big Brown breathed heavily as he pulled his great body with its large load. Ann took pride seeing Ginger prove to be an even greater weight-puller for her diminuitive size.

"We must seek a grist mill. I've not come this way before but Johnny Appleseed has directed me."

The trail often lay hidden in matted undergrowth and Jonathan must search for "blind signs" like an Indian. He studied the position of moss on the trees and on rare glimpses of sky, consulted movement of the sun.

A half-day's journey brought the riders out of the forests where before them lay a beautiful fertile valley. From the distance came a low rumbling sound. "It's the big wheel of the mill, grinding corn into grist."

In a green pasture several horses were feeding. A man came running toward the two riders aiming a rifle.

IV

Shelter From The Storm

"We're seeking the grist mill," Jonathan called out. The man lowered his rifle at once. "Howdy, strangers. Don't often see no lady in these parts and her a ridin' sidesaddle. The mill's up yonder but if'n you be bringin' corn, there's a three-day wait for the grindin'. You kin leave the horses here fer watchin'."

"Why do the horses need watching?" Ann asked Jonathan but it was the man who answered.

"Stealin' horses is a capital crime here in Ohio, Ma'am, but there be rivermen who risk it fer gittin' back north for work on another barge comin' back down the Big River."

"Rivermen?" Ann exclaimed. "Are we not a long way from the Mississippi River?"

"That be so, Ma'am, but it walks nigh 1300 mile to Pittsburgh from New Orleans and stealin' a horse sure beats walkin'."

Ann was unhappy at leaving Ginger but the horses were eager for the green grass. They pranced and capered until their riders finally turned them loose.

"That be a strange little filly you got there, Lady. I ain't niver seen the likes o' her. I reckon her muscles got power."

Ann and Jonathan walked back to the spring dammed to power the mill. They were greeted by a genial miller and a mixture of waiting customers—farmers, hunters and travellers—even a schoolmaster newly arrived at the nearest settlement. All had travelled a distance, some as far as forty miles, to bring corn to the grist mill. Most carried it in sacks slung over their shoulders. Those fortunate enough to own a mule or a horse had come walking, their grain sacks slung on each side of their animal.

"I takes one-fourth of the customer's grain," said the miller, "to pay for the grindin'."

At this harvest time of the year, the mill was running behind, but no one seemed to be minding the wait. Men and boys were gathered about the hopper. They busied themselves cleaning their ever-present rifles or sharpening their all-important axe with a piece of precious glass. They chewed on bits of parched corn as they swapped stories and news.

"This be good corn fer a husking bee," said one young customer. "It's good fer kissin' a girl ever time there be a red ear to shuck and yew kin see ez how this corn is plumb full o' red ears." The men laughed. Just then a newcomer collapsed on a rock.

"Wheew, I'm wore out fer the miles, but our baby's already on mush and milk and my woman had to pound the grist on a stump like an Indian squaw."

"Here, you kin have my turn. I only been here two days."

"Much obliged. I need to be gittin' back, fer my Missus ain't so good with the rifle."

"Be there Indians about? I hear there won't be no more Indians selling their lands. Chief Tecumseh's aimin' to unite all the tribes into a land-owning confederacy."

"Figurin' on Indians to one side o' the Ohio and white men t'other, I heered, but the tribes'll niver git along together. Tecumseh's got a brother folks be callin' The Prophet. What's he a prophet of, I'd like to be knowin'."

"The Prophet foresaw a darkening of the sky and it really happened the way he said it would. It was an eclipse of the sun."

"Say Mister, kin yew be the new schoolmaster?"

"Yes, I aim to teach a blab school this winter in the Chillicothe settlement. I'm passing the word to get pupils."

"Chillicothe white, or Chillicothe Indian?" asked the miller.

"Chillicothe white, of course," the schoolmaster answered. "The Indian camp is called Chalagawtha. That's Tecumseh territory. White men better stay away."

"You sure be knowin' a lot, Mister. What be you goin' to charge fer your blab school?"

"Two dollars a scholar for the term and I'll take room and board living with families around."

To while away the waiting, the schoolmaster took a book from his pocket and began to read. At the sight of a book, some of the men gathered about.

"I ain't niver seen a book 'cept the Bible," said one boy. "What does it say?"

The schoolmaster began to read aloud: "I met that bear in the woods and there I was with my rifle hanging back at the cabin. I found myself in a dangerous situation. . . ."

"What'd he do?" asked the excited boy.

"Don't interrupt," and the schoolmaster continued. "First I thought I'd climb a tree. But before I could do so, that bear kept coming closer and closer and closer. ." The schoolmaster looked around to find all the men listening. He went on reading: "The bear got so close I could feel his hot breath on my face."

"What'd he do, what's he do?" the boy interrupted again.

This time the schoolmaster ignored him. "I looked all about me," he read on. "There was no escape. So I just reached down that bear's throat and grabbed that bear's tail and turned that bear inside out. And that's the end of my *tale*, too." The schoolmaster yodelled and the men all laughed. "Kin I come to your school, Mister?" asked the boy.

Just then newcomers arrived—a frontiersman and his woman, leading a pack horse with all their plunder.

"Howdy stranger," the busy miller welcomed them. "Be ye travellin' or just goin' somewhere?"

"We be movin' to the Indiana Territory. We heered there be land good for pioneerin'."

"There's deep soil, all right, but don' build a cabin by the river. Them barges carry a crew o' boatmen. When darkness comes, they tie up to a stout tree and take off fer hellin'—'scuse the language, Ma'am."

"If those river hushers spot your cabin when darkness comes, they move in fer a night o' drinkin' and shoutin' and fightin'."

"Thank ye fer the warnin', friends. I allays heered what a bad lot the rivermen be."

"*Rivermen!* What be you sayin' bout rivermen?" a voice roared above the rumbling of the mill wheel.

All eyes turned to see a giant of a man with hair and beard standing wild, almost covering a pock-marked face. The man clung tightly to a jug of corn whiskey and weaved drunkenly as he spoke.

"I be a riverman," he shouted, slobbering over his bearded chin. He lurched forward unsteadily, splashing the contents of his jug, "and by God, I'll fight any man who speaks evil of my brothers of the barge."

The man raised his jug and struck a fighting stance that almost toppled him to the ground. The men laughed but the miller lunged to catch him and held him upright.

39

Ann clung to Jonathan. "Don't be upset, Ann. He's too comical drunk to make any trouble."

"You goin' north to catch another barge at Pittsburgh? How be you travellin', Brother?" asked the miller.

The riverman tipped his jug and drank deeply. "I got the cantankerous ol' mule you ever be wantin' to meet."

"A mule, huh! They ain't enough swear words in the hull language to gentle a mule fer ridin'."

Jonathan joined the conversation. "One day, you rivermen may not have to *walk* back north. I understand there's a boat being built with steam engines that can power it even against the strongest current."

The thick-speaking bargeman was still able to recognize a gentleman. "Say, Mister, be you the gent what claims that purty little mare yonder in the pasture?"

"Could you be referring to my wife's horse?"

"How'd you like to sell her? She's a strange lookin' horse as I ever seed. Holds her head like she's steppin' off in a parade." The Riverman threw back his own head to show how the mare looked and he staggered into the arms of the miller amidst the guffaws of the men. He pulled himself up proudly and checked his jug to see if it had lost any of its contents. "But I bet that mare's a powerful sprinter and I need to be travellin'."

"The horse is not for sale," Jonathan replied with firmness. "I told you it is my wife's horse."

"Your ol' woman's huh? I tell you what—I'll swap my mule for the mare. A mule's good enough for any ol' squaw missus."

Jonathan was angered. He raised his hand to strike him but Ann tugged on Jonathan's arm and the riverman cowered. He was last seen running into the woods still hugging his jug.

The only other woman put her arm around the trembling Ann. "I heered ye be from Indiana Territory, Ma'am. Kin ye tell what I kin be expecting?"

Jonathan proceeded with his business and the two women moved together in conversation. The woman offered to carry a letter and the busy miller obliged Ann with a turkey quill and ink made from the hickory ash. There was no paper so Ann wrote on a strip of birch bark: "Dear Mama. ." How she wished she could write of all the happenings and emotions of the journey, but there was space for only a message.

The chatter of the customers and the steady drone of the mill with its creaking buhrstones drifted over to her. She failed to notice the gathering of storm clouds over the trees. Nor did she see the Riverman slip stealthily past, heading for the pasture.

Jonathan completed his bargaining. "It's later than I thought. The miller has directed us to a friendly cabin for the night."

With exchanges of Godspeed, the Jennings walked to the pasture. Ann hurried, eager to be reunited with her beloved Ginger. Suddenly she stopped.

"Now what's holding you back?" Jonathan spoke crossly, still smarting from the scene with the Riverman. "We need to push on before dark."

"O Jonathan, I see Big Brown in the pasture but I don't see Ginger."

Then they both spotted the mare at the same time. She was munching contentedly, standing in Big Brown's shadow.

"Honestly, Ann, the way you carry on over that mare!"

At that moment they saw the watchman running toward them. "Mister, a drunken riverman tried to steal your lady's mare."

"Where, where is he?" Jonathan looked wildly over the pasture.

"It's awright, Mister. That big stallion o' yourn, he jest put his two forelegs on that riverman and knocked him clean over. The big horse would a trampled him, only the little mare, she whipped away fast off down the pasture n' the big horse took after like to see if she be awright."

Jonathan was enraged. "Where is he now? I'll settle him for good, and this time, no one will stop me." He glared at his wife.

"That bargeman was so scared he never got up. Jest rolled over on the ground till he reached the mule. He mounted that mule with cuss words that 'twas a good thing, Lady, you wasn't there to hear."

"O where is he now?" cried Ann.

"Wal he beat on that poor ol' jenny-mule to git her to go, until finally she took off like she had a burr in her tail-side."

"Which way?" shouted Jonathan ready to pursue the riverman.

"I don' think that mule had made up her mind yet," and the watchman went off into a laughing fit.

"It looks as if the stallion did your watchman's job for you. Anyway, here's a few fips for your service."

"Much obliged, Mister. It's looking mighty squally. You best be on your way."

"Come, Ann. The cabin the miller directed us to is not too far to ride." They mounted the two horses quickly.

"I'm frightened for Ginger. What if we meet the Riverman?"

"It seems as if you needn't be, with Big Brown to look after her," Jonathan spoke roughly.

The new path skirted the nearby woods until they came to a crossing of two trails. Jonathan hesitated. Now which one had the miller said would lead them to a friendly cabin?

The new trail plunged them once more into thick forests. The winds had strengthened and the trees stirred with a whine like the howling of wolves. Great gusts scattered leaves and twigs across their faces and tore at the legs of the horses.

As the storm closed in on the riders, thunder grew louder and lightning thrust jagged flashes silhouetting the tall trees like macabre giants.

Sparks crackled all about them when suddenly, a mighty thud shook the ground. Instinctive fear arrested Ginger in mid-gait and the mare faltered. The horse braced her forelegs as flashes of light revealed a fallen tree, still settling from its crash. The great tree, with its branches still swinging in weird patterns lay blocking the trail separating Ann from Jonathan.

Above the noise of the howling wind, Jonathan tried to direct Ann, clinging to Ginger's back. By the light of flashing firebolts, rider and horse struggled around the toppled giant.

"That was close," Jonathan shouted over the roar when they were once again at his side.

"Ginger saved me. Is there no shelter from the storm?"

"We should be nearing the cabin."

Then as abruptly as the storm had begun, there came a lull more foreboding than the fury. The wind ceased with a terrifying silence. Between lightning flashes, the blackness was complete.

Suddenly, Jonathan saw a small spot of light flickering through the shadows. A mighty explosion of lightning revealed a cabin only a few yards away. Over fallen branches and deep puddles they rode eagerly up to the cabin door just as a new outburst of wind and rain almost blinded them.

Dismounting with Ann close at his side, Jonathan pounded on the door, shouting, "Halloo-O the house!" Again and again he called out, pounding on the heavy door. At last, they could see that the latch was being slowly raised from within and the door was opened a few inches.

At first, they could see no one. Then a small boy came to the door holding a torch from the fire to bring light to the cabin room. Inside the door stood a woman pointing a rifle to bar the way. She stood, quietly staring at the travellers. She made no move to open the door wider.

After minutes that seemed forever as they stood in the drenching rains, the woman slowly lowered her rifle. With a claw-like hand she pushed locks of hair stiff as broom straw from her frightened eyes. Grimy-faced children peeked out at the strangers from behind the woman's ragged skirts.

"Madame, may we come in out of the storm? We saw your candle from the trail and were grateful for its guiding light."

The woman looked beyond them out into the storm as if expecting someone else but she opened the door a little wider. Still she made no gesture of welcome.

Just then the storm worsened into a crashing cloudburst and Jonathan gave the door a great push. The woman fell back in surprise and Jonathan pulled Ann with him through the door.

Ann rubbed the moisture from her eyes to find herself in such a littered one-room cabin that she almost wished she had stayed out in the storm. The children had run from the door and now stood huddled together near the loft ladder. The only light from the dismal fire showed their dirty clothes, hanging loose on pitifully thin bodies. They shuffled their feet in the dirt of the floor and their snuffling noses made the only sounds in the silence of the room.

She shivered from revulsion more than from her wet clothing, but when no invitation came to remove her cloak, she moved to the fire. The woman had laid aside the rifle but she made no move to perk up the bleak fire.

At last the woman spoke. "Be ye wantin' victuals? I kin manage."

Ann was hungry but she knew she could never swallow food in this filthy cabin at the hands of this piteous woman. Even Jonathan seemed not to have heard.

"May we stay the night?" he addressed her. "The storm seems not to be lessening."

The woman hesitated, then she nodded. Jonathan asked if there was a lean-to for the horses, but the woman shook her head. The storm abated a little and Jonathan left to see what he could do for Big Brown and Ginger.

Ann was left alone. She tried to visit with the woman but she got no response. The children huddled farther into their corner. Ann was relieved when Jonathan returned carrying their saddles and his rifle.

"I've tied the horses in a clump of saplings with some protection from the storm."

At that moment there came such a pounding on the door that the cabin shook.

"Open up!" came over the thunder. "Open up, Woman! Here's your man come home a-fetchin' friends."

The woman ran to the door. This time she opened it promptly and five very wet men fell into the cabin out of the storm. As soon as the children saw the men, they ran for the ladder to the loft. The woman hastened to build up the fire to full blazing.

The men shook the rain from their rough clothing like great wet dogs, making pools of mud on the dirt floor.

"Cripes, what have we here?" as they spotted Jonathan and Ann. The man recognized that the two strangers were gentleman and lady, and he bowed mockingly.

"'Scuse me, Ma'am, we ain't used to no 'ristocrats payin' us a visit. We be rivermen headin' back from the Mississippi! This here's my cabin and my woman."

"Rivermen! O Jonathan!" Ann whispered to her husband.

"We got caught in the storm and saw a light in your window," Jonathan spoke. "We sought permission from your wife to let us stay the night."

The man suddenly swung about and grabbed the woman's arm. "Who wuz you expectin', Woman? That light wuz fer me, warn't it?" The woman cowered from his threatening face as he twisted her arm until she cried out.

Jonathan hastened to speak, "I'll pay you well."

The man's eyes filled with a greedy gleam and he ordered the woman to bring rum for all. Jonathan joined the men as they took seats on benches beside the table near the fire. The woman shooed the peaking children up the ladder to the loft. She brought bowls of corn mush then from a great black kettle and placed a jug of rum before the men.

Ann stayed close to the fire to dry her clothing as best she could. At the table each of the men took a turn to tip the jug. When it was emptied, they pounded on the table until the woman brought another.

The jug was passed to Jonathan but Ann saw that he only pretended to drink. If any of the men noticed, they gave no sign. The jug would only remain the fuller for them.

The woman took a turn on the jug, too. Ann could have used a warming liquid but she was relieved that it was not passed to her. She watched the men scoop mush into their mouths sometimes with their filthy fists and she tried not to notice their satisfied belching.

She turned away and moved closer to the fire, trying as best she could to spread her soaked riding skirt to dry.

"Why don' you take it off, Lady?" The next thing Ann knew, one of the men snatched at her skirt as if to rip it from her body. Ann screamed. She tugged at her skirt to pull it from the man's grasp and fell back into the fireplace.

Jonathan was instantly at her side and grasped her from the flames. "Get to the loft," he commanded in a low voice. "I'll stay by the ladder."

"Don't make me leave you, Jonathan," Ann begged in a whisper.

"Do as I say!" Jonathan pushed her toward the loft.

Ann was as shaky as the rungs of the ladder she had to climb. She found the loft floor covered with sleeping children, snoring on dirty cornhusk mattresses. Ann crawled over the children as best she could to seek a knothole in the split logs of the floor where a tiny shaft of light shone through from the fire below.

She could see that all below were busy drinking and passing another jug. Soon they were fighting and brawling among themselves, screaming profanities and lewd language. They ignored Jonathan who stood at the foot of the ladder to the loft, pretending to be very sleepy drunk. His rifle was close to his hand.

The storm had commenced with renewed fury and the thunder claps became frequent and fierce. Ann worried about the horses. Once, above the roar of the tempest, she thought she heard the tormented cries of some animal in distress. It might be only the wildness of the wind whistling through the great trees. At last, the storm quieted and Ann heard the frightening sounds no more.

The hours passed slowly. One by one, the men dropped off into a drunken stupor to sprawl where they fell on the dirt of the cabin floor. The woman lay in the arms of the man who had clutched at Ann's skirt.

Ann wanted to call out to Jonathan but she was fearful that she might waken the rivermen.

The loft smelled of mold and mildew from the damp cornhusks in the mattresses and the odors of children's unwashed bodies. Rain dripped monotonously in leaks from the carelessly laid roof shakes. Ann lay very still at the knothole meaning to watch, but her eyes grew heavy and she dozed off.

In the middle of a nightmare, she wakened to feel a tugging at her skirt. As the pulling persisted, she came full awake to see in the half light of early morning, the shadow of a man on the ladder. She drew back in terror.

"SSssst, Ann wake up!"

Then in the thin light she distinguished Jonathan. He motioned to her to be silent, and she crawled cautiously over the sleeping children and down the ladder. Below all were snoring.

Quickly, they collected their gear and crept stealthily to the door. Jonathan slowly lifted the great bar that held it shut. Its rusty hinges grated as the door was opened. In the loft, one of the children cried out in his sleep, but the drunken slumberers snored on in a haze of rum as Ann and Jonathan crept from the cabin.

The night's storm was over. Droplets of water hung from the trees and all looked fresh and glistening in the lustre of a late moon mixed with early dawn-light. After so much violence, all was peaceful. The two made their way as quickly as they could under their heavy loads through dripping trees and deep puddles to the grove of saplings where Jonathan had tied the horses.

As they drew near, they heard a strange whimpering sound. Could this be the same sound Ann had heard over the storm? Then they heard it again. This time there was no doubt—it was the whining cry of a horse.

Jonathan dropped what he was carrying and began to run. Ann followed close at his heels. When they reached the grove where Jonathan had tied the horses, they halted in shock.

There stood Big Brown, but Jonathan could scarcely recognize his own horse. The stallion's proud head drooped. His tail hung limp. He neighed in soft cries like the sobbing of a hurt child.

Jonathan moved slowly toward the big horse, but Ann stood concreted to the path. Where was Ginger?

Close at the side of the drooping stallion stood a grotesque, head-hanging jenny-mule. Beside the mule lay a broken, muddied hat of twisted braided straw.

Ginger was nowhere to be seen!

V

Ann And The Jenny

Ann stood motionless. What was this poor misshapen animal doing here in Ginger's place! Suddenly she fell to her knees crying "Ginger, Ginger—where is my mare?"

Everywhere there was evidence of a mighty struggle. The earth at the stallion's feet showed the churning of hoofs in frantic pawing. The young sapling that held the rope from his halter was bent to the ground from his frenzied efforts to free himself. Even the roots of the tree were exposed where the great horse had pulled the sapling from the earth. Now the stallion hung his head in pain and defeat.

Jonathan examined the great horse. He found rope burns behind the horse's ears where he had pulled violently on his halter and deep scrapes where the branches of the tree scarred his flanks. But he found no major damage to the sturdy stallion.

With careful gentleness, Jonathan stroked the horse but when Big Brown nuzzled him gratefully, the master buried his head in the horse's mane and broke into shattering sobs. The sound brought Ann out of shock, and she rushed to Jonathan.

"I can't stand to see a horse mistreated," he tried to explain, embarassed at his display of emotion. "O Ann," as she held him close, "I should be comforting you, but I'll find Ginger if I have to ride every trail in Ohio."

"We'll find the mare. We'll leave at once." Jonathan spoke briskly now, once again taking command. But he reckoned without his wife's firmness.

"No, Jonathan. You're on your way to serve in the Congress, remember?"

"But Ann, we can't give up the search. I'll return to the cabin for help."

"Indeed no. I would not trust those drunken hushers. Let's take to the trail before anyone wakens. Ginger wouldn't make it easy for anyone riding her and they can't have travelled far."

"We'll take to the trail then, but we must find a way to carry our possessions. If you ride the pillion behind me, we can pack the jenny-mule."

"It's good you brought the saddles into the cabin. I'll be needing Ginger's saddle when we catch up with her." Ann was pretending to more confidence than she truly felt.

Jonathan moved to load the drooping mule but when he came near the jenny, she stepped out of his reach, braying loudly in panic. Jonathan was patient. He employed every strategy he knew to gentle the frightened mule. Finally in desperation, he pulled a strong twig from a nearby bush to make a whipping stick.

"This jenny's been treated badly. She's used to being beaten to conquer her stubbornness."

"She's not stubborn—only frightened. Here let me try."

Ann approached the mule quietly, speaking soft words in cajoling tones. She worked close enough to scratch the mule's long ears and rub the lean neck. She kept speaking nonsense words as she might to a frightened child. The mule stood quietly now and Jonathan placed the sidesaddle with the heavy bags over the lean bones.

But the saddle was too big and the poor mule too thin. She shook feebly and the saddle began to slip until it came to rest under the jenny's belly. Ann coaxed the mule quiet and gently placed the saddle once more on the lean back. This time it stayed in place.

"Let me try to ride her." Slowly Ann mounted the mule. She sat carefully into the saddle. But once again, the saddle came to rest under the animal's belly and Ann found herself at the mule's feet.

She wore such a surprised look on her face that Jonathan laughed. "Do you give up? We'd best make a pack mule of her. You ride Big Brown with me and we can lead her."

So they loaded the bags on the jenny and Ann sat behind Jonathan. At last all seemed ready. Big Brown turned and raised his hanging head to study the arrangements. He nickered dejectedly as if accepting this punishment for not saving Ginger.

The stallion started forward but once again they had failed to calculate the mule's determination. The animal planted her four feet obstinately on the ground.

"Giddap, gee-yup! . . ." Jonathan pulled on the reins and Big Brown plunged forward but the mule stood firm. Big Brown reared and Ann slid back over his tail until Jonathan reached out in time to keep her from falling into the dirt. It was difficult to determine whether Big Brown was too exhausted or the jenny-mule too stubborn. The jenny would not budge and the stallion could not.

"She's used to being ridden without a saddle. Let me try," Ann begged. Jonathan tossed Ann the reins in disgust. He removed all their possessions once again and the jenny-mule stood as if waiting for their next move.

As Ann approached her this time, the jenny brayed but the blast sounded less belligerent. Ann placed her saddle blanket on the mule and then with a tree stump for an upping block, she mounted lightly to sit with both legs dangling on one side.

But there was no pommel for Ann's knee and the jenny's back was boney. The blanket slid off and Ann with it. Once more, she lay on the woods floor. Had she ever worried about mud on her beautiful riding clothes?

This time, Jonathan did not laugh. "Are you hurt? Now, Ann, we must leave the mule behind and our possessions too, if necessary. We'll try to buy a horse to replace Ginger."

But where would they find a horse as fit for the journey as the little lost mare. Ann held back tears of frustration.

"There's one way I haven't tried yet. I'm going to ride the jenny the way she's used to being ridden."

"What are you doing?" as Jonathan watched her turn the apron of her riding skirt to bring the shorter side to her knees. "This is no time to be worrying about your muddied clothes."

To his amazement, Ann raised her skirt and flung a leg in its long brown pantaloon over the back of the jenny-mule. Arranging her clothes to cover her as best she could, she sat astride the jenny. The jenny flicked her big ears, swishing her tail with its single tuft of long hair at the end, and turned her great sad eyes on her new mistress.

Ann was used to the double pommels of her sidesaddle, but she gripped with her knees to keep her seat secure and the mule made no move to dislodge her. Ann raised her head high and smiled in triumph.

Jonathan was bewildered. No lady ever rode astride—nor even little girls who would one day grow up to be ladies and so must learn to ride sidesaddle.

"Don't be shocked, my husband. Mama once told us the story of a royal lady who made a bargain to ride through the streets without her clothes to save her country. She let her hair down to cover herself. Should I let my hair down?" Ann laughed uncertainly.

Jonathan laughed, too, then. "What a great lady you are!" He pulled on the reins of the stallion. "Gee-up!" This time Big Brown stepped out and so did the mule. They moved forward at last in a triumphant procession as the morning sun shone through the tree tops like a fanfare.

It was not too soon, for back at the cabin their absence would be noticed and the Jennings wanted no more of the rivermen and the woman.

With Jonathan's rifle ready across his saddle, they rode on at last, alert for a sound or sign that might reveal Ginger's trail. At a small stream, they thought they detected the mare's tracks but there was no sight of the little mare.

They rode as steadily as they could, stopping only when the boney back of the jenny made riding unbearable for Ann. Hour after hour passed until Jonathan grew convinced they were never going to catch up with Ginger and her thief.

"We must soon be out of the forest nearing the Pickaway Plains. There is certain to be a side trail to take us to the white village of Chillicothe where I'll try to buy another horse fit for the rest of the journey."

Ann turned away not to let Jonathan see her tears. All at once, the absurdity of their situation struck her and she began to laugh.

"Have you gone daft, Ann? What's happened now?" as he pulled up beside the mule.

"I was thinking how we'd look arriving at the Capital of our country.." Ann gestured dramatically from the back of the jolting jenny ". . . presenting the handsome Honorable Jonathan Jennings, Congressman-delegate from the great Indiana Territory, accompanied by his bouncing, beauteous bride on Jumping Jenny, the Mule."

Ann's humour was contagious and Jonathan was eager to share her good spirits. "Was ever a Congressman's wife in such a predicament?" Then he turned serious. "But then there never was a wife like mine—a wife who braves travel with courage and humour. I have indeed married a *very* woman."

"If my thoroughbred riding friends back in Kentucky should see me now!"

But as each mile carried them more remotely from the hope of finding Ginger, Ann found it difficult to keep up their spirits. She sang Johnny Appleseed's song and all the songs her Scotch-Irish mother had brought from Virginia. Big Brown began to improve even under his heavier load, but he often turned from the sight of the ugly beast in place of the beautiful mare.

The jenny-mule responded to the kind handling of her new mistress. She stretched her great ears at the sound of songs and laughter and seemed to step carefully for the comfort of the light load on her back. Still Ann was used to Ginger's easy gait and her muscles ached from the jouncing of the jenny. But her heart ached more as she began to doubt she would ever again see her beloved mare.

The trail took them through swamps and thickets. The animals kept their footing across rugged creek beds but travel was indeed slow. At the close of the day, Jonathan sighted a cave, its entrance almost hidden by brush and vine.

"This could be a place to stay the night. We need rest." But as he reined his horse before the opening, he observed fresh trampled brush and horse droppings.

He signalled Ann to stay back. With rifle ready, Jonathan dismounted and slowly approached the entrance. Suddenly, a single man emerged. He was leading a horse burdened with packs of trinkets and cooking pots.

"Put away your gun, Sir. I'm only a lonely peddler. I hid when I heard your horses. I thought you might be brigands."

Ann was both disappointed and relieved. No Ginger, but no fighting riverman either.

Then the peddler saw Ann sitting astride the mule. Ann blushed and pulled her skirt about her as best she could. The peddler had never before met a lady riding the wilderness and astride a mule. He looked away in embarassment.

"Are you truly a congressman, Sir?"

"Yes, and this is my wife." He told their story. "Could you have met our stolen mare on the trail?"

The peddler shook his head. "But I can bring you other news of the trail. You'd best avoid the Indian camp of Chillicothe," warned the peddler. "Many believe Tecumseh is really forming the confederacy to make war against the white man."

There was more talk and then Jonathan sought to make a trade with the peddler. "How'd you like to swap your horse for the jenny-mule. I'll pay you well."

"My horse is a pack horse. He's no saddler fit for the lady." He looked at Ann as if to question if she were truly a lady, riding astride as she was.

Ann spoke aside to Jonathan. "Don't be disappointed, I could never tolerate his old nag. I'm better off with poor Jenny."

The peddler moved on but the Jennings decided to bed down for the night as best they could in the damp cavern.

Ann lay awake a long time. She realized that Jonathan was facing concerns more serious than the loss of her mare. Would there really be war with the Indians? Was it true that Tecumseh could assemble an army of five thousand?

The peddler had also spoken of the scarcity and high cost of horses. Could Jonathan afford to buy her another horse? Ann turned and tossed on the damp cavern floor.

And what of Ginger? Was she never to see her little brown mare again?

The next morning the woods stretched monotonously before them. Not even the rasping kree-e-r squeal of a red-tailed hawk drew Ann's attention as it swooped low after some passing prey.

The trees grew closer and larger with the moldy thickness of years of leaves underfoot. Ann was struggling to keep the mule on the move, when suddenly the jenny stumbled. At the same moment, Ann saw the quiver of brush, and a shadowy form glided silently from behind a fallen log. There on the path, heading straight toward Ann and the mule, slithered an ugly reddish-brown copperhead snake, flicking a slender red tongue. Surprised by the hoofs of the animal, the snake raised its head with eyes peering through transparent skin and hissing jaws ready to strike.

Ann screamed in terror. Jonathan, only a few yards ahead, pressed his heels to turn Big Brown about at the same time he brought his rifle to aim. He saw the jenny lift her forelegs high but the poor mule was old and tired and the snake was fast. Its venom-carrying fangs punctured the mule's hind leg with the sharpness of a hypodermic needle. With a terrified bray, the jenny leaped into the air, and Ann slid off into the dirt of the trail.

Now it was Ann who lay in the path close to the copper-head's fangs. The snake reared back, ready once more to shoot the swift dart of its poison.

Jonathan readied his aim with great care but before he could pull the trigger, the snake dropped its jaw and fell back, writhing and twisting. As it squirmed and contorted its slimy body, Jonathan failed to see a flint-tipped arrow drop from the reptile's back.

He rushed to Ann's side where she sat hypnotized before the struggling snake. The copperhead gave a final massive shudder and turned its white belly to the sky. The snake lay dead on the trail.

Ann was safe but what of the poor jenny. The mule lay panting and twitching, her punctured leg already swelling as the quick-acting venom flooded through her blood stream.

"The poor jenny—can't we do something for her?" The mule writhed in torment and spasms of pain.

"It would be futile to apply a tourniquet. The poor animal will go into convulsions. I'd best put an end to her agony."

When Ann saw Jonathan aim his rifle, she turned away. Poor Jenny had been her friend in need. At that instant, the twang of a long-bow sounded through the trees and an arrow whizzed past close enough to make a breeze as it sliced the air.

The arrow hit its mark. The jenny-mule lay in peace. The entire episode had taken place with such swiftness that Jonathan had overlooked the arrow that killed the copperhead, but now he was aware that arrows shot with such accuracy might come only from the strong bow of an Indian.

Yet where was the unseen archer? Jonathan looked cautiously about. He listened for the sound of moving twig and rustle of leaf but he heard nothing and saw no shadows. Could the arrow have come from one of the tall trees whose great butts walled in the trail?

He looked up. A flash of color moved in the high branches above. At the same moment, an Indian warrior appeared before Ann on the trail. Jonathan moved quickly to her as another Indian slipped softly from behind the wide trunk of a tree. Then another and another appeared from hidden ambush until Indians surrounded Jonathan and Ann on all sides.

The warriors stood tall and erect, blocking the trail. Their copper-colored bodies were covered only with the buckskin breech cloths of the Indian hunters. Their hair had been shaved into scalp-locks for the hunt to prevent entangling with bush and branch. In their scalp-locks were fastened feathers of honor signifying deeds of great bravery. From their belts dangled sheaths holding flint-tipped arrows and tomahawks. Each brave stood beside a long hickory bow as tall as himself and held a flint-tipped arrow.

Climbing down from the top of a tall tree came still another Indian. This one bore the markings of a chieftain of the hunt, wearing the four-feathered headdress of honor. Now, he too, confronted the travellers. With his great bow at his side, he stood menacingly before them.

Not a word passed among them. One of the Indians stepped to the slain snake to recover the arrow fallen from its back. Another pulled out the arrow that had put the jenny to rest. They cleaned the arrows in the leaves and returned them to the Chief-of-the-Hunt who had shot them from the tree.

Jonathan stood fearlessly with his arm protectively about his wife. He met the eyes of the Chieftain with poise and courage. Ann knew that Indians respect bravery in others as well as in themselves and she tried not to show her fright. She had heard of captured white girls being adopted into Indian tribes. Had they killed the snake to save her for capture? Would she be taken from Jonathan?

Silently one of the Indians took Jonathan's rifle from him. There was no struggle. Both knew resistance would be futile. Their possessions were removed from the dead jenny. With gestures, the Chieftain ordered them to accompany the Indians on foot.

One Indian seized Big Brown's reins but the horse threw all his wits and strength against him. He tossed his powerful head, wrenching the bridle from the surprised Indian. The great stallion reared and bucked until Jonathan himself stepped forward to quiet the horse. No one stopped him as he took hold of the reins to lead Big Brown into the march as the Indians began the running walk of the Shawnee.

Running beside the horse, Jonathan was well-guarded but no notice was paid to Ann. She was left to follow as best she could. In and out of the tall trees through the rough underbrush, she tried bravely to maintain their fast pace. At first, she tried to place her tiny-booted foot into the moccasined footprint of the warrior ahead as she saw the Indians do. But the brave was six feet tall with the strong legs accustomed to the running walk of the hunter. His arms hung close to the ground as his body leaned forward in easy gait.

Ann's heavy riding skirt dragged at the bushes to hold her back. She was a good runner but she soon fell behind.

"I must keep trying," she sobbed to herself. "I must not be separated from Jonathan."

When Jonathan saw that Ann was being left behind, he stopped on the trail. He sent for the Chieftain and insisted with words and gestures that Ann be permitted to ride the horse.

The Chieftain studied for awhile. Then the young man spoke, "We are Shawnee. Shawnee walkers. Squaw ride mule. Now no mule. Squaw walk."

"I am Jonathan Jennings, Congressman from the Indiana Territory. This is my wife. We go to Washington to see the great White Father."

"Chief Fleetheels know who you are, know your mission."

"You know who I am?" Jonathan spoke in surprise. "Then you must know that my government will not like hearing that one of their officials has been treated with discourtesy."

The young chief listened but his face remained passive. He spoke no words. Then abruptly he cupped his two hands to his mouth and uttered a blood-curdling cry. The strange whooping sound was caught up by the next warrior in the line. Then the next Indian and the next repeated the yell until the forest seemed to ring with hundreds of voices.

Jonathan knew that some message was being communicated and that the file of Indians must stretch far ahead. Without waiting for consent, he quickly mounted Ann on the stallion and then turned defiantly to the one who called himself Fleetheels. No one stopped him and the procession began to move forward again.

The wild whoops had subsided like the closing notes of an echo. Soon there were only the sounds of the forest and clumping hoofs of the great horse. The Indian hunters stepped swiftly in their noiseless moccasins as if stalking some animal for the hunt.

Changes in the forest became visible now as tree trunks were smaller and spaces of sky bestowed light to the woods. The trail itself began to widen and straighten, giving visibility ahead. A second time some echoing message was repeated along the trail but softly this time and the Indians came to an abrupt halt.

57

Jonathan welcomed the pause after running at the side of Big Brown but what did this stop mean.

From her high post on Big Brown's back, Ann strained to see, when through the new quiet, came the sound of a woman's voice. A haunting melody floated through the forest stillness.

The mournful sound grew louder and came closer, but still there was only the one voice. Then through the trees, Ann caught sight of the lonely figure of an Indian woman standing at the foot of a tall tree. She was dressed in the long tunic of the Shawnee and as she chanted the mournful melody, she swayed gently from side to side as if rocking a baby in her arms, always looking to the top of the tree.

A breeze parted the leaves and Ann saw high in the tree a small pen fashioned with crossed logs like a tiny cabin. It was built over a child's cradle board. Tied snugly to the board that could keep a baby's back so straight in life were the remains of a dead child.

"That poor woman is singing to her dead baby. She is all alone? Help me to dismount, Jonathan. I must go to her."

"No!" Jonathan spoke firmly, holding Ann to the horse's back. "Indians respect the privacy of mourning."

High in the tree the little cradle with its log-cabin cover swung gently in the breeze. All at once, the mother's song changed to a cheerful lullaby and the Indian words drifted to them:

Wauwau tay see! Wau tay see!
E kow a shin!
Tshe bwan ne baun e wee
Be eghaun-be-eghaum-ewee!
Was sa koon ain je gun. Was sa koon sin je gun!

"Why she sings the chant of the firefly like Mama," and Ann began to sing the same melody with her mother's words:

Firefly, firefly! Bright little thing!
Light baby to sleep while gently I sing!
Give out your light as you fly overhead
That baby may joyfully sleep in her bed!
Come, little candle, that light up the night
Bright little fairy-bug, give us your light.

There were tears in Ann's eyes as she sang when suddenly she was aware that the one called Fleetheels was at her side. He spoke gently, "Little obbinijee only a bud—ka-ga-osh—on flight to higher air. Bright White Flower daughter of Sweet Breeze, now with great Spirit. Is no grief."

This was the first speech from Fleetheels and somehow it seemed to make him less fearsome. Jonathan would have liked even to question the young chief. Where are our captors taking us? What will they do to us? But he knew that Shawnee respect good manners and to question Fleetheels would be impolite. So he held his tongue and warned Ann to do the same.

The march began again. As they passed the bereaved mother, the Indians chanted softly. "Ta-no-kiah, ta-no-ki-ah, (farewell) Ka-ga-osh! Ta-no-ki-ah!"

The Indians resumed their running walk but Ann continued to ride Big Brown. Her feet dangled sideways too short to reach a stirrup and she missed the pommels of her own saddle. She clutched the big horse's mane to keep her seat on his broad back but now she could see the long file stretching far ahead.

As they moved downward from the high ridge, she could see that all seemed to be loaded with game. Some carried deer tied by their four feet to poles supported from shoulder to shoulder. Others were loaded with small game—rabbits, squirrels, and quail.

She spoke low to Jonathan. "Indians don't kill for the sport of killing," Jonathan explained. "They must be preparing for some great feast. Before they kill, they even explain to the animal's spirit that his body is necessary for the food of life."

Presently the trail began to widen. Trees were slender and spaced farther apart so sunlight penetrated the forest creating patterns of fillagree. For the first time in many days, the Jennings came into the full brightness of a noonday sun.

There before them stretched a broad green valley outlined by the graceful curve of a river shimmering in the sunlight. "This must be Pickaway Plains and the Scioto River," said Jonathan as they blinked against the sun's bold stare.

The wigwams of an Indian camp lay across the River. From the distance, it looked like a toy village but it was real enough, filled with uncertainties for the two prisoners.

"What will they do to us?" Ann spoke in a whisper, for she was uncertain how much their captors could understand. "I've heard terrifying tales of the Shawnee. O Jonathan, I'm so frightened for us."

59

"Tecumseh has banned torture of prisoners. But we must be approaching the Sept of the Chalagawtha where Black Hoof is village chief. I've had dealings with Black Hoof and I've found him to be a friend to white men."

They began to descend rapidly now from the high ridge. The trail looped steeply in horseshoe pattern in and out of grass and growth, sloping toward the river. Here the long grasses turned into muck of swamps along the river's shores.

The foremost Indians crossed the narrow waters, wading or swimming, but those bearing the large carcass of an animal poled across on small rafts like the one Jonathan had ferried the day of Ginger's first swim.

The Indian guards led their prisoners to a shallow crossing where Jonathan was allowed to ride on Big Brown with Ann. She held fast to Jonathan as the big stallion waded across a sand bar. "Please don't let them take me from you, please, please!" she whispered.

As they came closer to the Indian village, they could see the wigwams where the Indians lived clustered in a great circle. Each rounded wigewa* wore a roof of brown bark like a wig with a hole in the top to let smoke escape from fire inside.

They watched the long file of hunters welcomed on their return but they were met with seeming stoic indifference as the women carried the game to their wigewas.

Approaching the encampment, Ann saw horses grazing in a distant pasture. "I thought Shawnee do not have horses. Will they take Big Brown from us?"

Suddenly, from the distance came a loud whinny. At the sound Big Brown lifted his head. His ears began to twitch and Ann could feel his skin quiver. Jonathan had already dismounted but Big Brown tossed his head so vigorously that his mane pulled from Ann's grasping fingers, and she slid into her husband's arms.

The neigh came once again like a call flung across the field. With frenzied strength, Big Brown pulled his reins from the surprised Jonathan and broke free with a mighty leap.

With his tail straight out and his ears laid back, the great stallion plunged through the tall grasses. Indians came running

---

* Wigewa—a special type of wigwam.

60

from all sides but none were fast enough to reach the horse as he galloped past.

Ann and Jonathan stood transfixed. The Indians, too, stood spellbound. Never before had they seen anything like the big horse's break for freedom. To have restrained the stallion would have been to grasp at the wind.

There had to be something very special to excite such wildness in steady Big Brown. The whinnying cry came again and this time, Ann, too, left Jonathan's side. She began to run after Big Brown and no warrior tried to stop her. She lifted her riding skirt high and paid no heed to watching Indians amazed at the sight of the running white woman and her long pantaloons.

Ann ran as fast as when she used to race her brothers. The surprised Jonathan recovered in seconds and he began to follow her flying feet. They arrived at the pasture together.

There at the far span of the pasture stood a small brown mare. The little horse was pulling hard on the grapevine rope that restrained her, dancing and pirouetting about like a circus horse to reach the big brown stallion.

Big Brown drew close, and the mare neighed joyously. She nuzzled Big Brown and the tall stallion pushed affectionately at the mare's shaggy mane. They wiggled ears and rubbed noses.

Suddenly the mare raised her head. Ann stood close but she made no move. Then simultaneously, horse and girl gave her own kind of cry. Ann rushed to embrace Ginger and the mare rubbed her sturdy shoulders against her mistress. Ann mixed sobs with whispers as she spoke into the mare's twitching ears.

Jonathan stood scrutinizing the little horse and was relieved to see that her appearance was sleek and healthy. The mare showed signs of excellent care.

With the arrival of his master, handsome Big Brown seemed to recall the dignity of his position as saddle horse to a congressman. He held his head high recovering appropriate behavior, but his intelligent eyes shifted forward and sideways to follow the young mare's every exciting movement.

Jonathan turned sharply from enjoying the picture of Ann reunited with Ginger when he became aware of Fleetheels at his side.

"Mare holds worth?" the chieftain spoke. "Horse groomed good. Fed grains and grasses."

"Indeed, indeed! She belongs to my wife and is greatly admired by Madame Jennings. But the mare was stolen—how did you come by the horse?"

Fleetheels drew himself up to his great height. "Shawnee not steal. Village Chief waits. Come!"

"I know your village chief. I will meet with Chief Black Hoof."

"Black Hoof not of Sept of Chalagawtha. Black Hoof of Sept of River Auglaise while Chief Tecumseh is gone south."

Jonathan tried not to show his disappointment.

"Chief Great Horned Owl waits for man and squaw. *Now!*"

His words were a command, but Ann clung to Ginger as if she were afraid the mare might disappear again. She finally turned to Jonathan expecting to see him sharing her joy but she saw that his face looked troubled. At his side stood the one called Fleetheels.

At that moment, a handsome young brave approached Ginger and began to stroke the mare with great love and gentleness. Ann was surprised to see how the mare welcomed the boy's attention. She sensed some affectionate relationship between the boy and her beloved mare.

But now she heard Fleetheels speak. "Chalagawtha Sept of the Shawnee gather for corn festival. Fires of the past made dark. New fire from sticks rubbed together, gift of new year. Scotach— (pointing to the Indian gentling the mare)—carry gift of new fire to farthest clan of Shawnee. Only Scotach tell what befell him on way. Chief Great Horned Owl waits."

This time Jonathan knew that they must go to meet whatever fate awaited the two captives.

VI

Mare-Of-The-Autumn-Moon

So joyful at finding Ginger, Ann forgot she was still a prisoner. She knew she had no choice but to leave Ginger for now, but at least the two horses were reunited when Big Brown was left in the pasture with the little mare.

A full guard of Shawnee led Jonathan but only Fleetheels walked at Ann's side. He was courteous but firm. They crossed an open field where the maize was already in the harvest and women were tending late-summer gardens. The camp looked so peaceful that Ann felt some of her fear subsiding. Even the Indian children were too shy to stare at the two white captives.

They came finally to a great circle of wigwams where they were taken to one larger than all the others. Before it, on a low platform, shaded by an awning of woven bark, sat the dignified figure of a distinguished Indian.

He was richly dressed. His robe was of the finest deerskin, ornamented with fringes and beadwork. His leather leggings were lavishly embroideried with dyed straws and quills. His girdle was rich with wampum of polished shells and beads. His belt held the carved wooden handle of a hunting knife with a sharp flint blade. On his head, he wore the four feathers that spoke of bravery. Around his neck hung a pendant bearing the emblem of his clan. It was easy to see that here was an Indian with the blood of chieftains in his veins.

The guards pushed Jonathan forward. When Ann saw this, she broke from Fleetheels and ran to stand beside him. Matching the dignity of the Indian chief himself, Ann and Jonathan stood together before him.

After a pause that seemed long to the frightened Ann, the Indian chief raised his arm and spoke one word—"Nickah!"

Jonathan recognized the friendly salutation. With a nod, he, too, raised his arm and answered, "Nickah—Friend!"

In the language of the white man, the Indian chieftain began to speak. "Chief Great Horned Owl greets Congressman Jennings."

"You, too, know who I am?" blurted Jonathan.

But the Chief continued as if there had been no interruption.

"Like the great horned owl who is feathered king of the forest, Village Chief is fierce and powerful here in the tall timber." He paused for the effect of his words.

"I understand that you are powerful here in the forest," Jonathan interrupted, "like the great horned owl whose name you bear. But if you are aware who I am, you must know that with my people, I, too, am strong and powerful. Why, then, do I stand before you a prisoner? Why have your hunters taken me from the trail?"

Chief Great Horned Owl made no reply but turned instead to Fleetheels and gave orders in the language of the Shawnee. Fleetheels disappeared into the wigewa and returned bearing a long Indian pipe which he passed to the Chief. The flame-colored bowl of the pipe was lavishly ornamented with the carved heads of birds and flowers. Fastened to the middle of the long stem, bright-colored feathers spread out like a fan.

Great Horned Owl rose now and stood before them. Holding the calumet in his two hands, he began to chant. He pointed the pipe to the west and to the east. Then he turned it up to the sky and finally down toward the earth as he continued to chant: "Ai-ia-ae-, hai-ha-aiee!"

Presently he drew a deep intake of smoke from the pipe and with more Indian words, Chief Great Horned Owl passed the calumet to Jonathan and waited.

Jonathan did not understand the words nor did he know what was expected of him, so he imitated what the Chief had done. With his two hands holding the pipe as he had seen Chief Great Horned Owl do, he chanted the words of a prayer. He, too, pointed the pipe first to the west and then to the east, and to the sky and to the earth. At the close, he shouted, "Hallelujah, Hosanna! Peace from the Great Spirit of all mankind."

The watching Indians gave no sign as Fleetheels took the pipe of friendship from Jonathan. Great Horned Owl took a seat on the ground and motioned to Jonathan to do the same. Ann too was permitted to sit close by. She had not understood what was happening but she was relieved that the pipe had not been passed to her.

Others came now to complete a circle. They wore the insignia of clan chiefs of the village council of the Sept. When all were assembled, Fleetheels passed the pipe from one to another.

After each had smoked, Great Horned Owl once again began to speak. This time he employed the cultivated English of a learned Indian chief who had long associations with the white man.

"We come to the season of the Keeghingwaa," he spoke, "August-Fit-to-be-Eaten-Month that ripens into harvest. Wild geese soon fly south. Winter moon comes, maybe snow moons. Shawnee are industrious, crops are abundant."

The Chief spoke with the formal high-pitched voice of an orator: "To the brave belongs the forest: he hunts, defends his clan, seeks the blessings of the Spirits. To the squaw belongs the wigwam: she cultivates the fields, carries wood and water, raises children. In the world of heaven and earth, Shawnee braves and squaws share.

"All the long summer," the Chief continued, "men dance to call on the rain to make the plants grow. Now the Great Spirit will hear gratitude for abundance of corn ripening into harvest. As our fathers before us, we go to prepare for Festival-of-the-Green-Corn."

With the close of his speech, all the Indians rose and departed each to his own wigewa.

"What will they do with us?" Ann whispered. "Could we run for the horses and reach the trail?" but Fleetheels was instantly at their side.

"Rites of hospitality sacred to Shawnee," he spoke. "Highest seat for visitors. Come to lodge of Chief. Prepare for Festival."

Jonathan took Ann's arm but Fleetheels shook his head. At the same moment, a beautiful young maiden stood at Ann's side. She spoke with English words. "Bright Cloud take white squaw to wigwam of Grandmother."

"I wish to go with my husband," Ann spoke firmly, but she saw Jonathan and Fleetheels disappear into the lodge. Two Indians stood guard.

"Who are you?" she asked of the Indian girl.

"Bright Cloud to marry with Scotach who care for Mare-of-the-Autumn-Moon. Bring Scotach good will of Spirits."

"Do you speak of my mare called Ginger?"

"Bright Cloud know. Mare bring feather of bravery to Scotach—feather of eagle." Bright Cloud spoke proudly.

"Feather of eagle?"

"Is honor feather—second feather of manhood. Scotach marry now with Bright Cloud," and the Indian girl hung her head in shyness.

"O was it Scotach who found my mare? How did he find Ginger?"

"Story belong to Scotach. Bright Cloud prepare for Festival-of-the-Green-Corn." and she started toward the wigwams.

Ann looked back. Two stalwart Indian warriors were watching her. Would they stop her if she tried to follow Jonathan? Bright Cloud took her hand and they moved across the circle with the guarding Indians close behind.

In the meantime, Fleetheels had escorted Jonathan to the lodge where both men must stoop low to enter the dome-shaped wigwam. The Indian signed for Jonathan to do as he did. They removed their clothes and he gave Jonathan a breech cloth like his own.

Jonathan felt very white beside the handsome bronze body of the Indian as he saw Fleetheels study the skin of the white man. The chieftain motioned Jonathan to follow and together they ran through the woods to a nearby creek where the Indian immediately plunged into its clear waters. Jonathan followed but his body shivered at the unexpected chill.

He copied Fleetheels' actions as they scrubbed and splashed in the clear-running stream, shielded by waving ferns and marsh grasses. They dried quickly in the warmth of the sun and Jonathan felt invigorated and restored.

Running swiftly once more through the woods, they returned to the lodge. It is easy to see, thought Jonathan, why Fleetheels bore his name well, for his heels flew with the swiftness of quicksilver.

Jonathan was surprised to find that his clothes had been brushed clean and all his possessions returned—all except his rifle. But now the young chieftain held out a beautiful leather hunting shirt. "For you."

Jonathan felt the softness of the tanned fawn skins. He fingered the intricate beadwork and the fringed hems.

"Is the Corn Festival so sacred that your captive, too, must be so richly attired?"

"Shirt is gift of Scotach. Bright Cloud make from skins of hunt."

"Who is Scotach?"

"For Scotach, you are servant of Great Spirit. Horse called Mare-of-the-Autumn-Moon bring good fortune."

"Do you speak of the mare belonging to my wife? Where have you taken Madame Jennings? White men tolerate no harm to their women."

"Festival season now. Great Spirit protects prisoners. Honored guests of Chalagawtha for Festival."

"And after the Festival?" persisted Jonathan.

Fleetheels shrugged. "It is not yet spoken."

With these words, the young brave walked from the wigwam. For the first time since their capture, Jonathan found himself alone. Should he try to find Ann? Should he try to take the horses and make an escape?

Outside the wigwam, he saw the two Indians standing guard. Hospitality for visitors takes no chances, he thought. He lay down finally, on the old buffalo skin rug spread for him on the dirt floor of the lodge. He prayed that Ann, too, was receiving kindness.

Jonathan woke to the sound of two voices outside the lodge raised as if in argument. When he heard Madame Jennings named, he crept to the door to listen.

Chief Great Horned Owl was speaking angrily to Fleetheels. "Madame Jennings may not be taken for squaw to Fleetheels. Congressman Jennings is important to the Great White Father in Washington. It is decreed by the Council that he be guest of the Sept for the Festival."

"But after the Festival?" Fleetheels spoke. "White woman is *my* prisoner. Fleetheels saved white woman from the copperhead on the trail. Fleetheels captured the woman."

"No! If woman be kept against her will, white man could make war with the Shawnee. Chief Great Horned Owl is opposed to war between Indian and the white man. Seek another for your squaw."

"Never has Fleetheels sought favor from Village Chief. Has not Chief-of-Hunt provided well for Festival with spoils of the hunt for the feasting? Has not Fleetheels always followed the Council in Powwow? White squaw of much beauty and bravery.

Grateful to be adopted into tribe to be Indian squaw of one who saved her life."

"The will of the Council has been determined. It is decreed that Madame Jennings be guest of Festival. The favor of the Congressman is sought to take new treaties to Washington."

"Fleetheels must respect the decree of the Council. To obey with honor will be difficult."

Jonathan watched Chief Great Horned Owl walk away as Fleetheels approached the lodge. He gave no sign that he had overheard the alarming conversation. Fleetheels spoke only one word, "Come!"

Ann followed Bright Cloud through the village. The strange-looking wigwams were made of saplings bent to form arches and covered with squares of bark woven together like carpets. The roofs were tied down with strips of basswood to hold them from ripping winds. Ann could smell the fragrance of wood smoke as it escaped from the square holes in the center of each roof.

Before each wigwam, platforms stood high on stilts, holding deer hides and meats drying in the sun. Outside the wigwams, returning hunters had already hung the tails of animals as offerings to the departed spirits of the animals.

Women and girls were busy sewing with needles of bone or preparing food. A cradle board hung on the back of a woman as she worked, but this board held a live baby. It was tied snugly to the board with toys of beads and bones dangling brightly above as the baby nestled content and close to his mother.

At the farthest wigwam, Bright Cloud stopped. "This is the wig-was-i-ga-mig of Grandmother. Come."

Children were playing a game before the wigwam. "These are brothers and sisters to me," Bright Cloud introduced; "Annenakens (Little Thunder), Welungee (Little Turtle) and Tung-lungle (Smallest Turtle). Muangreet (Big Feet) is eldest. Ann knew she must not smile at the strange names.

The children were playing with dice made from the pits of the wild plum tree. They were painted black on one side and white or yellow on the other. Welungee shook the dice in a clay pot and the others shouted a guess which color would turn up on the throw.

Bright Cloud explained. "Huts, huts—white. Honesy, honesy is yellow. Rego—black."

"Black—REGO?" asked Ann just as the black side of the pit turned up. The surprised children looked up. Ann laughed. "Did I win?" as Muangreet scratched marks in the sand.

"They have little white man talk," Bright Cloud spoke as she led Ann into the wigwam.

After the bright sunlight, the interior seemed as dark as the forests. The only light within came from the cooking fire in the center of the room, where two women squatted on the floor.

"Grandmother. Other Mother," introduced Bright Cloud but the two women made no reply. Grandmother went on sewing decorations on a beautiful white robe made from the skins of the rare albino deer. It was delicately embroideried with bright colored beads and dyed porcupine quills. She was adding more quills which she took from a clay pot where they were soaking. She clinched each one between her teeth to flatten it before sewing it to the resplendent robe.

Both Grandmother and Other Mother were dressed in simple tunics. Their hair was twisted into club braids, wrapped with thongs of dyed buckskin. Ann sensed that the women were too polite to show their curiosity but she felt no hostility in the wigwam. If this were to be her prison, Ann found it more interesting than alarming.

As Ann's eyes became accustomed to the dim light, she saw that a wooden platform about two feet off the dirt floor ran about the sides of the wigwam. Bright Cloud filled a gourd with water from a large clay pot setting on this platform. Then she led Ann behind a screen made of animal skins and gave her the water for washing.

Ann was grateful. While she washed, she watched Bright Cloud make up a bed on the narrow platform. First she placed a mat of woven rushes and then covered it with a blanket of soft deer skins. When Ann was clad once again in her undergarments, Bright Cloud led her to the bed and covered her with a robe of beaver and fox skins.

From her strange bed, Ann watched as Other Mother swept the dirt floor with a broom of grass and carefully shovelled ashes from the dirt into a box made of tree bark. Ann lay very still and comfortable. Without meaning to, she drifted into sleep.

When she wakened, the day had moved closer to sunset. Ann sat up confused to find the three women standing over her. They were elaborately dressed now. Grandmother and Other Mother wore robes of deerskin made rich with embroidery of beads and shells. On their arms they wore many bracelets, and ear bobs dangled to their shoulders.

Bright Cloud stood resplendent in a robe made from the softest fawn skins. A beaded headband across her forehead held back her waist-long hair. It was tied in a heavy club braid wrapped with ribbons of many colors.

"O Bright Cloud, you look like a princess!" Ann forgot to be frightened of the three women watching her so closely.

Bright Cloud cast her eyes down shyly, "For marry with Scotach."

But the three women moved away at once and spoke together in syllables of the Shawnee. Then Other Mother, followed by Bright Cloud and Grandmother, came to Ann, bearing the exquisite white deerskin robe Ann had seen. Together they slipped it carefully over Ann's head and Bright Cloud laced the slender buckskin thongs across her shoulders.

On Ann's tiny feet they placed elaborately beaded moccasins that fit as perfectly as the glass slipper on Cinderella. Other Mother combed Ann's long hair with a brush made from a porcupine tail. Bright Cloud worked the heavy hair into two thick braids weaving into each a scarlet buckskin thong dyed with the juice of the blood root.

Then without a word, the women stood back shyly as if waiting for the girl's approval.

Ann stood entranced. She turned and twisted to finger the dainty embroidery of beads and quills. How she wished for the tall pier glass at home or even the looking glass from Sam Blish's cabin. But she stepped and pirouetted about, delighting in the supple doeskin as soft against her skin as the silk of her wedding gown.

"The robe is lovely—it makes me feel beautiful," she spoke at last. Suddenly her face clouded. "Why have you dressed me this way? Are you making me into a Shawnee? Am I to be kept here in the Indian camp forever?"

Ann was suddenly very frightened. She was tired of being brave. "Where is my husband? Please take me to him," and tears came into her eyes.

Through her tears, she saw the faces of the three women. Their usually expressionless faces showed bewilderment and disappointment.

"It's a beautiful robe," Ann hastened to say minding her manners, "But it is Indian. I do not wish to be Indian."

Bright Cloud spoke now. "Do not be afraid. Dress for Festival-of-the-Green-Corn. Robe gift of happiness. Wear for marry of Bright Cloud with Scotach."

"O Bright Cloud, if I have misunderstood, I am ashamed. But please, please, Bright Cloud, will you not take me to Congressman Jennings?"

The three women looked at each other. Then Grandmother spoke for the first time. "Now!" and she led them from the wigwam.

VII
Festival-Of-The-Green-Corn

As they emerged from the wigewa, two Indian guards were waiting. Grandmother led the way. Bright Cloud and Other Mother followed but the Shawnee guards stayed close on either side of Ann.

As the little procession passed through the village, Ann saw that the wigwams were empty. Many Indians were assembling from all sides to the steady beating of distant drums.

"Scotach carry gift of fire to other septs. Invite to Festival-of-the-Green-Corn. Many come," explained Bright Cloud.

The braves were dressed for the festival celebrations. Faces were vividly painted and many wore head feathers of green, orange-red, and yellow. Shirts were of skins embellished with designs of shells and quills, and trimmed with the teeth and claws of animals. Hung from belts in leather sheaths were buckskin pouches for carrying extra arrows and sharp-edged flint knives.

Many carried tomahawks that made Ann cringe when the sharp blades flashed wickedly in the sunlight. The Shawnee braves were prepared for festival or war.

The squaws, too, were brilliantly clothed but Ann saw no maiden as lovely as Bright Cloud in her doeskin robe. Nor did Ann see another white tunic of the albino deer like the one she was wearing.

In contrast to the bright colors, the faces of the Indians were solemn and unsmiling. It was impossible for Ann to tell if they were friendly, for they took no notice of her.

But where was Jonathan? Suddenly, across the space she saw him. Was it really Jonathan wearing an Indian shirt? She started to run toward him but the two Indian guards grabbed her. She struggled to break free but she was no match for the sturdy braves. They held her captive, as one held on to her arm.

Why had Jonathan not come to her? Had he not recognized her in the Indian tunic? She was determined to reach him. She would watch her chance. Suddenly, a running child stumbled against the Indian holding her arm. He lost his grasp and before he caught her, Ann was off and away. The loose-fitting robe didn't

73

weigh her down like her riding skirt. She twisted easily and lightly in and out through the crowd of surprised Indians.

Then abruptly she stopped. Jonathan had disappeared. She stood confused until she felt someone coming close behind her and she started running again. But the one who followed her was fleeter still.

It was Bright Cloud. "Why do you run? White Horse and Big Beaver take you to husband. Trust Bright Cloud."

Ann was angered. "If you would have me trust you, tell me what is to become of me?"

Bright Cloud answered. "Shawnee speak little. Wait!"

Ann sighed. She would have to learn patience with these people, but her guards disappeared, and Bright Cloud led her to join Grandmother and Other Mother.

The many Indians,—braves, squaws, and their children, were seated now making a great circle about a council fire, blazing brightly in the center. Ann saw Jonathan again. He was seated at the right of Chief Great Horned Owl and beside him sat Fleetheels and the Indians of the Village Council.

"Stay!" commanded Bright Cloud as once again Ann attempted to join Jonathan. They took places across from him where at least Ann could be aware of his movements. Bright Cloud spoke shyly. "One beside Fleetheels is Scotach. To marry with." It was the same Indian boy who had stroked Ginger so fondly.

From across the wide circle, Jonathan spotted Ann. He saw that she, too, was wearing Indian dress. How beautiful she looked he thought, with her lovely red-brown hair in braids over her shoulders. But what did this mean? He hoped that it was a sign that Festival hospitality had been extended to her also. But what was to happen when the Festival was over?

At that moment, the drums stopped their monotonous pounding and the crowd waited in hushed silence. Chief Great Horned Owl rose. With noble grace and dignity, he stood before the crowd in all his ceremonial robes.

"The Council Fire of the New Year flames," he began. "It is time to give thanks to the Great Spirit for the year that has passed." His strong voice cast the syllables of the language of the Shawnee to the farthest listeners.

Bright Cloud tried to explain to Ann as the Chief continued speaking. "From the trail, returning hunters bring visitors to Chalagawtha. There is story to tell. It is story of Scotach."

Scotach rose to stand before all. He looked very young and handsome in his festival finery with his scalp-lock neatly braided. He began to speak in the language of the Shawnee. Many times before, the Sept had heard his story but they listened proudly.

"What is he saying?" whispered Ann.

"Story of Scotach will be twice-told. First-Teller-of-Tales speaks, too."

This is the story in white man's words as told by First-Teller-of-Tales:

> To Scotach was given honor of carrying gift of new fire to farthest clan of Shawnee. In days of August moon, Scotach ran through the forest trails, taking care never to let the flame go black. His mission accomplished, the great Chief Tecumseh himself, bestowed upon Scotach First-Feather-of-Bravery.

> Scotach was eager to return to his village to tell of his good fortune. Returning through criss-crossed trails of the forest, Scotach looked up one day to see a great flock of birds on the ridge. Suddenly, the birds took off in flight. Quickly, Scotach climbed the tallest tree to see what had scared birds into the air. Looking down he spotted a white man and a small brown mare. Man in great anger was flogging the horse with his leather belt. The mare screamed in pain and terror. Scotach watched the little horse try to escape from the man's blows but strong thongs hobbled the mare's feet.

As Ann listened, her eyes filled with tears. Could this have been her beloved Ginger? The story-teller continued:

> Shawnee are land-travellers—hold great respect for horse. Scotach climbed quickly down and began to run from tree to tree, hiding in ambush waiting for the chance to save the mare.

> The ugly man gave the little mare a savage kick. Scotach could wait no longer. With a wild

yell, he made a mighty leap to the man's shoulders. Taken by surprise, the huge man fell to the ground with Scotach on top of him. The two rolled over and over. They grappled and struggled amidst the terrified screams of the mare. At last the man broke away from the grasp of the young brave but when he tried to get to his feet, he staggered and fell back with a bellow of pain. The man's head struck a sharp boulder and he lay still. Blood poured from the man's head. Scotach held his tomahawk ready to strike but the man never moved. Never again would he abuse another horse.

Scotach left the man beside his whiskey jug and turned eagerly to the mare. At first, she whipped away from him. She snorted and trembled as Scotach's gentle hands removed the hobble from her feet. Then she let him lead her along the trail till they came to the water from a clear spring. He washed the mare's abrasions and applied healing herbs from the woods to comfort her. The horse studied the Indian boy. At last, she rubbed her head against his arm and Scotach was beside himself with joy. How could such an evil man have come by this wonderful horse?

Scotach slipped his blanket over the horse's back. When he tried to mount her, the mare was jumpy, but he held an easy rein and the mare settled into a short-stepping trot that was almost a dance.

What would be spoken when he returned to the sept riding this beautiful mare Scotach wondered. He hoped the Council might even let him keep her and he named her *Mare-of-the-Autumn-Moon*.

It was a dramatic homecoming for Scotach. Not only was he wearing the First-Feather-of-Honor from Chief Tecumseh himself but he came riding a magnificent mare. But even before he could tell his story he was ordered to the lodge of the Village Chief.

Chief Great Horned Owl called the Council
of Elders to powwow to hear the story of Scotach.
When it was learned how Scotach had saved the
wonderful horse from certain death, the council
awarded him the Second-Feather-of-Bravery.
Scotach was filled with joy for now he could hold
marriage with the beautiful Bright Cloud. Now
the story of Scotach is told.

Ann saw Bright Cloud's happy face and she shared in her
delight. "Why, I am friend to an Indian girl!" she thought.

But the Council had permitted Scotach to keep the mare
only if the real owner of the stolen horse never came to claim her.
Scotach had rejoiced, for it was unlikely that a white man would
come to the proud Shawnee village seeking a stolen horse. He
cared for the mare, feeding and grooming her with affection and
tenderness, until one day a Shawnee scout had returned to the
Village. He brought news of the capture of the white man's chief
and his squaw. He told the story of the mule, and Fleetheels
himself had sent word that the horse Scotach had rescued was
certain to be the stolen mare.

"Should he bring the two captives to Chalagawtha?"
Fleetheels had asked.

"Bring white chief and squaw to Chalagawtha," it was
decided by the Council, "for the Congressman Chief is known for
fair dealings with Indians. If his mare is returned, the white chief
may carry new treaties to his Great White Father in Washington."

So Scotach must give up Mare-of-the-Autumn-Moon. "It
will be as the Council of my elders has spoken," the disappointed
Scotach had promised.

None of this had been revealed to the prisoners but now the
story of the mare's brave rescue had been told. The Indians had
listened spellbound as it was spoken in the strange tongue of the
white man.

Jonathan was deeply moved. He addressed Chief Great
Horned Owl, "Does this mean the mare is returned to us? Are we
free to continue on our journey?"

Chief Great Horned Owl ignored the question. "It is the will
of the Council," he spoke, "that the second feather of honor for the
brave Scotach be the feather of an eagle."

A sigh of approval spread softly through the great circle. "By such token," the Chief continued, "Scotach is accepted into full manhood in the Shawnee totem to learn all things passed on to him from his elders."

Still he had not finished. "It is the will of the Council that Madame Jennings bestow this Feather-of-the-Eagle on Scotach who saved her mare."

A soft whisper swept through the watching circle of Indians but before Ann could recover from her surprise, the young brave stood tall before her.

Fleetheels passed her the feather to be presented. "However will I reach his headband," Ann wondered as she looked up at the proud brave with his head held high. But Scotach knelt before her, his eyes almost on the same level as her own.

She fastened the feather of the bird of the wilderness in the honor headband of this boy who had saved her mare as the great circle of Indians watched in silence.

Ann did not know that this was the first time a white woman had ever performed such a ceremony of honor for the Shawnee.

Then Bright Cloud was brought to stand at the side of Scotach and Chief Great Horned Owl spoke once more. "I ask the Great Spirit to bless this marriage." As the two stood side by side, he spoke these words:

> Now for you there is no rain,
> For one is shelter to the other.
> Now for you there is no sun,
> For one is shelter to the other.
> Now for you there is no night,
> For one is light to the other.
> Now forever—forever, there is no loneliness.*

Jonathan watched Ann's eyes fill with tears as he stood now at her side. Was she moved by the beauty of the prayer? Or was she sad for the young brave who must yield his right to Mare-of-the-Autumn-Moon? Jonathan would find no answer to his questions for Ann herself could not have told him.

---

* Salish Indian Prayer of Marriage translation, courtesy of *The Province*, Vancouver, British Columbia, Canada.

At the close of the prayer, the circle of Shawnee continued to sit motionless, waiting for the Chief to speak again.

"Summer ripens into autumn. The Great Spirit, Father of us all, has been generous—harvest abundant. We dance to his glory."

"Now are we free to leave?" Ann whispered to Jonathan as the great circle rose as one. But before he could respond, Jonathan was led away by the Chief himself and Ann found herself once again guarded by White Horn and Big Beaver.

Many drums began to throb like the sound of waves beating on a rocky shore. With inscrutable faces, men, women, and children began to shuffle to the accents of rattling gourds and the tinkle of bells and buffalo tips suspended from boots and leggings.

The circle moved forward clockwise as the Indians swayed and stomped to the beat of sticks slapped on folds of heavy hides. Sounding over the beat came whistling from wooden stick-flutes like the birds of the forests.

"Whee-e-au, whee-e-whaigh, whee-e-au, whee-w-whaight," the leader chanted and the dancers answered in unison as they stomped. The single line wound round and round toward the center as tight as a ribbon rosette. Then with shambling step, the long line slowly began its unwinding to once again form a far-flung circle.

Standing between White Horn and Big Beaver, Ann watched, fascinated by the intricate stepping but she was not invited to take part. The dance was a reverent ritual belonging only to the Shawnee.

The Indians began to stomp faster and faster. They raised knes to chins, twisting and turning in ever-increasing frenzy. As tomahawks waved and gourds rattled, the pulsating pattern of the drums grew frantic until Ann became fearful.

Jonathan had disappeared into the Lodge of Chief Great Horned Owl. Bright Cloud was in the dancing circle. Suddenly Ann became aware that both White Horn and Big Beaver had vanished. For the first time since their capture, she was alone. Could she make a run for the pasture to Ginger?

At that moment, she felt a tug on her sleeve. She turned quickly. Big Feet and Smallest Turtle stood timidly at her side. With round dark eyes watching her, they pointed to a small circle of children. Grown tired from the dancing, the children were playing games. They were inviting Ann to join them in a game of hide-the-pebble.

Each child placed his moccasins on the ground before him. Big Feet was chosen to move about the circle, pretending to place a pebble in each moccasin. They kept careful watch to try to guess whose moccasin received the pebble. Ann placed her lovely pair of new moccasins before her to participate in the game but she was never fast enough to detect the pebble's hiding place, nor were her moccasins ever chosen.

Many games spread over the camp now as the dancing came to an end. Both adults and children played kick ball with bare feet and a splintery ball. "Your feet must be as tough as Johnny Appleseed's," Ann spoke aloud but no one understood.

Smallest Turtle rolled hoops over the ground for others to try to throw sticks through the hoops as they rolled past. Running races were popular and Ann was amazed to see how swiftly the Indians could run. Fleetheels was the fastest of all.

She watched him as he taught some of the older boys to aim blow-guns made from hollow reeds. They blew arrows of light wood through the guns with great accuracy. Fleetheels himself blew an arrow that snuffed out the flame of a candle ten yards away. Ann congratulated him.

"Blow-gun take practice and patience," explained Fleetheels. "Make boy good hunter, good warrior."

"Is that how you acquired such perfect aim when you killed the copperhead?" she asked. "You may have saved my life, you know."

The Indian Chief-of-the-Hunt turned away. "What if your arrow had missed its mark?" Ann persisted.

"Shawnee never waste arrow. Shawnee never miss," and Fleetheels walked away abruptly.

Ann felt a tug on her skirt. She looked down to see a tiny Indian girl holding out a small doll fashioned of corn husks, made fast to a cradle board. She wanted Ann to place the papoose-cradle on her back the way her mother had carried her when she was a baby.

As Ann fastened the buckskin straps about the tiny shoulders, a woman came to take the child away. Ann recognized her.

"You are Sweet Breeze. I heard you in the woods singing to your dead baby. I was saddened for you."

Sweet Breeze studied Ann and then using the white woman's language with difficulty, she spoke, "Great Spirit take Bright-White Flower to higher air of heaven." She raised her eyes toward the sky. "No grief. Only loneliness. Have Morning Star," as she pointed to her little girl.

Just then, Ann saw Jonathan crossing the clearing and she ran eagerly to meet him.

"O Jonathan, what did the Chief say? Will he let us leave now?"

"Not so fast, Ann. Chief Great Horned Owl spoke only of relations between the Indian and the white man. Tecumseh has gone south to urge the Choctaws and the Chickasaws to unite with all the tribes in an Indian nation."

"I don't care about Tecumseh. What about us? Are we to be kept here until they get what they want?"

"We must learn patience from the Shawnee. They will speak when they are ready. The Chief believes Tecumseh's way is the path to war. He seeks for me to take the threats of war to Washington and hopes I can arrange further treaties."

"And if he doesn't get the treaties? Am I to be kept here as a hostage? They have dressed me like an Indian! O Jonathan, I am afraid."

Jonathan recalled the conversation he had overheard between the Chief and Fleetheels and he took Ann into his arms.

"Nothing could make me leave you behind—nothing!" and he held her so close that the beads and quills on her Indian robe pressed into her flesh.

Indian women were everywhere, carrying great trenchers of food. Bright Cloud and Scotach came to lead them to seats of honor and Grandmother herself began to serve them. Other Mother and Bright Cloud, too, brought bowl after bowl filled with food—fish fresh caught from the Scioto River, juicy pieces of deer meat from the hunt, corn bread made from the fine meal of the white maize. They were even given two-tined forks crafted from the bone of an animal.

"Eat up, Ann. The Shawnee consider it an insult to leave food in your bowl."

Still the women came with more fruits of the abundant harvest—corn cakes wrapped in cabbage leaves that had been buried to bake in hot ashes, squash dripping with fresh sweet honey, puddings of pumpkin and sweet potato, and gourds of pure cold spring water.

"I could use some good corn whiskey to wash it down," Jonathan spoke softly, "but the old Chief forbids spiritous liquids in his sept."

"Jonathan, is Shawnee hospitality sacred only during the Festival? What is to happen when it is over?"

"Do not be worrying," he answered between mouthfuls. Ann sighed. No situation seemed so grim that it disturbed Jonathan's appetite.

Feasting and social dancing continued about the great blaze of the new fire. Sunset had long since cast its radiant red glow over the Festival. The great autumn moon rose now above the silhouetted shadows of the forest trees and shone orange-red over the valley.

"Will the celebrating never be done with?"

Fleetheels had come up silently behind them. "Harvest plenty. Much time needed to thank Great Spirit. Festival-of-the-Green-Corn many days."

"They will keep us prisoners here forever," Ann spoke softly to Jonathan. "They will never let us go."

"Fleetheels said 'many days' for the Festival. We are indeed fortunate he didn't say 'many moons'."

But the sensitive ears of the Indian caught their words. "Tonight sleep in lodge of Chief. Early light of morning white man leave on journey."

For one golden moment, Ann forgot that she should not display emotion before the dignified Shawnee. She clasped her husband in jubilation.

Fleetheels spoke angrily. "Bright Cloud come for white squaw," and he strode off into the blackness of the forest.

"Did he say *man* go on journey? What of me? Can't we run for the horses and leave at once while they are busy with the celebration?"

Just then, they saw Bright Cloud running toward them.

"Go with Bright Cloud. Tomorrow will bring us together, God willing."

82

The Indian guards were still nowhere to be seen. Only Bright Cloud led Ann to the wigewa. "Will you not be in the wigwam of Scotach this night?" Ann asked.

"When Scotach-of-the-Eagle-Feather prepares new wigewa, Bright Cloud go with him," she smiled shyly.

At the wigwam they found the little brothers and sisters fast asleep, cozy and cunning in fuzzy blankets of rabbit skins, but Grandmother and Other Mother were still at the Festival.

In the glow of the dying fire, Bright Cloud unlaced the ties of Ann's beautiful Indian robe. She folded it carefully into a packet of doeskin along with the moccasins and the beaded headband.

"For you. Gift to wear in good fortune. The Great Spirit will bring peace and plenty."

"It is a beautiful gift and I shall cherish it always."

Ann wished she had something to give her new friend. She could pack so few possessions in her saddle pouch but she carried a bracelet of sea shells which had come from the Virginian shores of her mother's birthplace. "The bracelet could make good wampum, daughter," her mother had told Ann, "for Indians believe that shells of the sea have a mystical power to bring good luck."

Ann drew the bracelet from her pouch and caressed the shining band that held the shells together. Could she bring herself to part with the treasured bracelet? Yet was not Bright Cloud the bride of Scotach who had rescued her beloved Ginger?

She hesitated no longer. "This is gift for you."

Bright Cloud looked at the delicate bracelet with its wondrous shells of the sea and her eyes filled with tears.

Ann was dumbfounded. "I thought Indian girls never cry."

"Only from joy," Bright Cloud spoke in a whisper. "Is good that Indian girl and white girl be friends," and the two embraced.

Ann slept well that night in her nest of soft skins. Grown accustomed to the darkness of the ancient trees, she was surprised to waken to a sun already shining with the pink glow of dawn.

She was alone in the wigwam. Water had been drawn and her riding clothes, somehow cleansed of their mud and travel stains, were carefully laid out along with the packet holding the Indian robe. She hastened to dress.

When she hurried from the wigwam she saw neither White Horn nor Big Beaver. Was she to be free at last? Many Indians were still assembled about the Council fire. But where was Jonathan? Could it be that he was still being held captive in the lodge of the Chief?

Then she saw him waiting for her. He stood with Big Brown and Ginger, groomed and saddled for the journey. Ann's joy was complete. Once again she ran lightly across the field.

The two horses neighed and nickered on Ann's arrival, stepping about in their eagerness at being reunited with their riders.

Chief Great Horned Owl approached accompanied by Fleetheels. At the same moment, White Horn and Big Beaver rode up on small ponies. Ann was alarmed.

Fleetheels spoke, "Big Beaver and White Horn escort Congressman Jennings to Flint Ridge. There leave Indian trails. Make way on white man's Trace." With these words, he turned abruptly and walked into the woods.

Ann wondered if she would ever meet the handsome young brave again. She was satisfied to have thanked him yesterday for killing the copperhead.

But Chief Great Horned Owl still had words for Congressman Jennings. "We set you free to take Shawnee message to Great White Father in Washington. Many moons ago, the Great Spirit made the earth, the air, the clouds, the seas, for the free use of all his children. Many moons they lived contented. Now white man is greedy for Indian domains. Tell your Great White Father how it is with us."

Then the Chief removed the handsome pendant he wore about his neck. It bore the design of the great horned owl, king of the forests. "This is symbol of Shawnee totem. Keep it as token of the Chalagawtha Sept where Shawnee hearts can be as strong in friendship as in hate."

Jonathan accepted the pendant and paid his respects to this wise chief so against war for his people. "I can make no gift of white wampum to signify new treaties that I am not empowered to make, but I promise to carry your message to Washington."

The Jennings mounted their horses and saluted farewell. They barely touched heels to Big Brown and Ginger who took off eagerly. Big Beaver and White Horn followed closely.

When the riders reached the ridge they had descended with such fearful anxieties, Ann brought Ginger to a halt, and looked back at the Chalagawtha camp.

In the shade of a great oak, she saw an Indian brave and a maiden standing side by side. As the two raised their hands in an Indian salute of friendship, something bright from the arm of the woman caught the sparkle of the sun.

Ann spoke softly, "Farewell, beautiful Bright Cloud! To-no-kiah, brave Scotach! Thank you for Mare-of-the-Autumn-Moon."

She touched Ginger lightly with her heels and did not look back again.

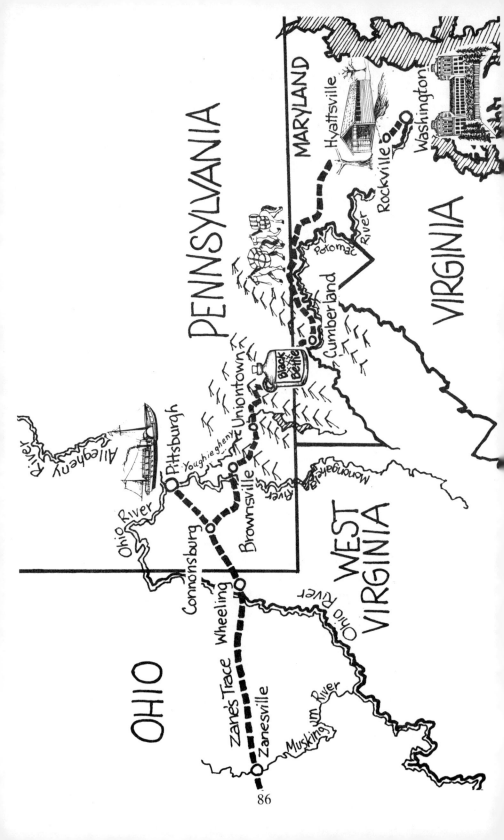

OHIO

WEST
VIRGINIA

PENNSYLVANIA

MARYLAND

VIRGINIA

Allegheny River

Ohio River

Pittsburgh

Connonsburg

Youghiegheny River

Brownsville

Uniontown

Monongahela River

Black Bettle

Cumberland

Potomac River

Hyattsville

Rockville

Washington

Zane's Trace

Wheeling

Zanesville

Muskingum River

Ohio River

VIII

Tolls, Taverns, And Travellers

White Horn took the lead with Big Beaver following the captive riders. Neither Big Brown nor Ginger took kindly to the two ponies but the trail soon narrowed to one-horse width through a thick-timbered world.

At the first widening, Ann pulled alongside Jonathan.

"Are we never to be rid of the Indians? Maybe they'll rob us or steal Ginger. Can't we ride away from them?" She spoke with lowered voice for she never knew how much could be understood.

"Be brave a little longer, Ann. The Chief will hold to his promise to have us escorted as far as Flint Ridge. The Indians are after flint, not us."

"What do you mean?"

"Indians come from hundreds of miles to Flint Ridge. They believe the flint from the pits there makes the fastest arrowheads and the sharpest knives. Anyway, at Flint Ridge we will be on sacred ground."

"Sacred ground?"

There was no opportunity for Jonathan to explain, for at that moment, the ridge trail opened to a view of the flint cliffs. Before them, stretching for hundreds of yards near the river, was a huge quarry.

As they rode closer, they could see many Indians of different tribes at work in the pits. Some were chipping stone with tools looked to be made from the sharp antlers of a deer. Others were shaping the quartz into arrowheads and tomahawk blades. Flint against flint made sparks fly.

Overlooking the pits, White Horn and Big Beaver pulled up and gave signs to dismount. With no word spoken, they squatted on the ground and began to eat food from their bag of provisions.

"We have food, too, thanks to your friend Fleetheels."

"*My* friend! You mean because he saved my life?"

"Huh! I could have killed that copperhead with one shot. Anyway he wanted to keep you for his squaw. I overheard him trying to claim you. Fortunately, Chief Great Horned Owl had other plans for me and holding you would have endangered them."

"You didn't tell me."

"And scare you? I wouldn't have let it happen—even if we had to fight it out like the story of that black hand on the side of the cliff over there."

"Where? I see only a black rock. What do you mean, Jonathan?"

"Well, the Indians tell that years ago there was so much fighting over the flint here that the Great Father told the tribes he made the flint for the use of all and he designated this ridge as sacred ground. He ruled that there be no more blood shed at the pits and promised a curse on any tribe that might ever violate this sacred place."

Jonathan was already chewing on pieces of deer meat as Ann persisted, "But what of the black hand you pointed out? I don't understand."

"That black rock is said to be really a hand cut off one of the two braves who fought on this sacred ground for the love of an Indian maiden. They all fell into the River and were drowned. The hand grew into that big black rock you see there to remain forever a reminder of the curse."

"How romantic but how sad. But why did Fleetheels want to keep me for his squaw?"

Jonathan shrugged. "Probably respected your bravery. And he found you to be almost as fleet as Fleetheels himself."

Ann watched the Indians chipping on the flint. How sharp the arrowheads looked. How would they be used? To aim at the birds of the sky or the animals of the forest? Or pointed at the white man? "Good hunters make good warriors," Fleetheels had said when he told the boys with the blow guns to practice. She was grateful to Fleetheels for killing the copperhead but to become his Indian squaw—Ann shuddered. Perhaps next time she might not be so fortunate if she were captured.

The two Indians had finished eating and rose as if to join their captives. Suddenly they saw that Big Beaver was pointing a rifle. Jonathan was instantly in front of Ann protectively, but he had forfeited his gun when they were captured on the trail.

Together, the two Indians came closer, Big Beaver still holding the rifle. After what seemed a lifetime of minutes, he lowered the rifle and held it out to Jonathan.

Taken off guard, Jonathan stood reluctant. Then he saw that the rifle was his own.

"Nickah," he spoke and the Indians gave the salute of friendship.

Without a word, they mounted their ponies and rode off, leaving Jonathan and Ann alone. Ann gave a cry mixed with relief and joy and she clung to Jonathan. Over her shoulder, Jonathan noted that the Indians did not take the trail back to Chalagawtha. He watched them join, instead, the many Indians in the pits.

If Tecumseh could truly raise an army of five thousand, he was thinking, the arrows of the warriors would be plentiful and sharp, but Jonathan spoke none of this to Ann.

Hastily they took off and soon were riding a new trail, marked with the white man's blaze. "Indians scorn the white man's need to blaze trees to mark the way." Jonathan explained. "They are taught to follow Nature's signs."

"Then who marked the trail with the tree-notches, Jonathan?"

"This is Zane's Trace made years ago by a famous Indian fighter named Ebenezer Zane. He and his brother faced great hardships and dangers to build it."

"It won't take us past another Indian camp, will it?"

"Zane's Trace brought so many settlers to the territory that the Indians pulled out, forced to find new hunting grounds—enough settlers to make Ohio a state. See what happens when there's a road? If only I can make the Congress see how a national road could bring emigrants to Indiana!"

As the trace took them from the deep woods, they began to meet up with other travellers. Most rode horseback or led pack horses and mules loaded with goods. Once Big Brown and Ginger were forced to the side of the Trace to let a family-loaded wagon pass. Unused to trail-traffic, Big Brown as usual stayed steady but Ginger was skittish.

They came to a log bridge where Jonathan paid the tollkeeper six and a half cents each to let them take the horses across.

"Goodness, to travel the Trace will be costly," exclaimed Ann.

"Congressmen are allowed six dollars a day for travel costs. Tonight we'll stay at Nye's Tavern just beyond Zane's village. He has separate sleeping rooms for privacy."

"No shivaree tonight?"

Jonathan laughed. "This is Ohio. I don't have voter-friends in Ohio."

They reached Zanesville before dark. "This looks to be bigger than the village of Madison," Ann exclaimed with excitement.

"Wait till you see Pittsburgh. There's said to be five thousand people living there. That's more people than in our whole Indiana Territory." Jonathan sighed unhappily.

They rode through the village to the doors of Nye's Tavern, a popular stop on the way to the East.

"I'm sorry, Congressman Jennings, you're too late," said the tavern-keeper, "unless you and the pretty Missus wants to share. We got four beds in a room and one's not spoken for."

When the taverner saw their crestfallen looks, he spoke again. "Taverns set close on the Trace. If you can ride another four mile, you'll be seein' the sign for the Hope and Anchor. The stage sleeps there."

Once again they mounted Big Brown and Ginger. "What did the innkeeper mean—'the stage sleeps there'?"

"It's where the stage coach stops to change horses and the passengers spend the night. I fear this Inn will be crowded, too."

Tired riders and horses rode grimly on. It was almost dark when they saw the picture-sign of an anchor with a real iron chain dangling from it. Ann was too tired to become excited at her first sight of a three-story building. But they were in luck for they were given a room to themselves and good stabling for the horses.

All was quiet. Travellers who spend weary hours riding over roads as rough as corduroy retire early. The late arrivals were served a good meal. Then they, too, retired to a comfortable bed.

"O Jonathan, I pray nothing happens to separate us ever again. Hold me close, Jonathan."

And Jonathan did.

Ann woke the next morning to the clamourous clanging of a deep-toned bell. "Come to breakfast," someone was shouting. "The stage coach is due."

Ann was surprised to see that Jonathan had already gone below without waking her, so she hastened to join him in the Commons Room where she found him eating breakfast with several strangers at a long pine table.

He came to her at once and introduced her to a distinguished gentleman who bowed with great gallantry. "This is my friend, Henry Clay. We'll be serving in the Congress together. He's come from Lexington by post horse and will board the stage here to ride on to Washington City."

"I am delighted to meet Congressman Jennings' lovely bride." He spoke with a deep musical voice. Ann had heard of Senator Clay whose wit and charming manners had made him a popular figure in her birthstate of Kentucky. "Indeed, Madame Jennings, you must be the first to make such a dangerous journey to accompany your husband to Washington City. You are a brave lady."

Ann curtsied as she thanked him in her soft drawl so like his.

"Your new home in Lexington is said to be a show place, Senator Clay," Jonathan spoke. "And are you not to be congratulated on the birth of a son?"

"Yes, thank you. Henry Clay, Junior was born in April and we had need of Ashland to house our growing family, but I'll have to wait for more houses to be built in Washington City before my family can accompany me. Our new Capital has well earned its nickname of City-of-Streets-Without-Houses."

"Or the Capital-of-Miserable-Huts," added Jonathan. "I am afraid we'll be forced to seek lodgings in a boarding house like the other congressmen."

"Still the greatest difficulty in serving in the Congress lies in the journey," spoke Mr. Clay. "Last year when I served in the Senate, I left Kentucky in October. I rode post horses until I reached the Ohio. Then I travelled up the River on a keelboat until we became trapped in a storm. I didn't reach the Capital until December. We could certainly use that east-west road we were discussing, Congressman Jennings—all the way to the Mississippi."

Ann listened wide-eyed. "I'm satisfied to be travelling with our own horses."

"Yes, one of the most distasteful problems of the journey," continued Mr. Clay, "was the prolonged associations with the boat crews of the River."

"You mean rivermen, Sir?" interjected Ann.

Jonathan told the story then of their mare's theft and now the other men at the table stopped to listen.

"Sounds to me like you met up with ol' Evel Earthquake," one of the men broke into the conversation. "He's mightier and tougher than Mike Fink, king of the keelboats." With his mouth half full, he burst into song: "He's a Salt River roarer half horse, half alligator; suckled by a wildcat and a playmate of a snapping turtle. . ."

Senator Clay interrupted. "Come, my good man, you are in the presence of a lady and the song grows ribald."

"I apologize, Ma'am, but those rivermen are a rough lot. Folks tell as how Evel Earthquake got his name 'cause when he walks ashore, the whole earth quakes under him. Ha, ha!"

The diplomatic Mr. Clay turned the conversation into other channels. "We're fortunate indeed to be here at the Hope and Anchor. One night I was forced to lodge where my bed kept slipping down until I propped it up with the fire tongs."

"Onct," added the singer, "I slept where the landlord kept a puttin' more and more folk into my room. Come mornin' I woke up to find five a sleepin' in my bed."

"All males, I reckon," said another who, after a haughty stare from the gentlemen, hastened to add, "I got outa bed one night, only 'twasn't people what druv me out—'twas bed bugs—scratch, scratch!"

This time it was Ann who interrupted. "Senator Clay, will you enjoy serving in the House this term instead of in the Senate?"

Before he could answer there was a great commotion outside the tavern and the silvery sound of a horn echoed from far down the Trace.

"The stage is a comin'! The stage is a comin'!"

The taverner hurried to strike a large iron triangle to sound the warning. Children and grown-ups came running from all sides to see the dramatic arrival.

Two men waiting to board scrambled to collect their possessions. A lone woman passenger came from the Inn carrying several handboxes followed by the landlord dragging her large portmanteau.

With the sound of pounding hoofs and mighty shouts from the driver, six matched horses, their harnesses shining in the sun, galloped into view pulling the handsome stagecoach.

Mud clods and dust splattered the waiting crowd as the driver brought the massive horses to a sharp halt at the very door of the tavern. Never had Ann seen such horses so powerful and so expertly handled.

Two coachmen sat high on the outer seat, one with strong hands held the reins of the six horses while the other sat with a ready rifle across his knees.

Out of the confusion and jumble of people and noises, baggage and cargo were quickly stowed on top of the handsome painted coach. A mail-pouch was passed up to the armed driver. The lady passenger had to be boosted up the high steps. Her long skirts dragged on the wheel and her travelling veil caught on the door knocking her bonnet over her eyes.

"It looks easier for a lady to mount a horse without an upping block than to board a coach," commented Ann.

"It makes for a mighty rugged ride for her, too, at seven miles or so every hour, over tree stumps and corduroy log roads."

Henry Clay was squeezed in now along with the other passengers. Even on the velvet plush seat, he looked mighty uncomfortable with his knees drawn under him.

"Don't forget, Congressman Jennings," he called out, "I'm on your side about that east-west road. Perhaps together we can make the Congress recognize our needs. Madame Jennings, Ma'am, I look forward to meeting you again in Washington. We may all find quarters in the same boarding house. You would be a charming addition, Madame Jennings. . . ."

Before he could finish, the driver cracked a great whip long enough to reach to the foremost pair of lead horses. With a tumultuous shout from the driver, the six horses lurched forward throwing Henry Clay back in his seat. The stage coach jolted off over the ruts and ribs of the strip-log road, almost hidden in a great cloud of dirt and dust.

Onlookers melted into the surroundings and the excitement was over till the next time.

"I like Senator Clay. Does he practice law in Kentucky when he's not serving in Washington?"

"Yes, but he also owns rich farm lands in the blue grass country and more than fifty slaves."

"He holds then with slavery?"

"Henry Clay is a good politician. He believes that for the good of the nation, the number of states for and against slavery should be equal. When it comes to a new state like Missouri, he believes in compromise—half the state for slavery and half the state free."

"Will Indiana come into the Union as a free state someday?"

"If I have anything to say about it! No man ought to be slave to another."

"And no woman?"

Jonathan nodded. "And no woman."

Leaving the Hope and Anchor, the horses crossed the riffles and shallows of the Muskingum River. Ginger took her cues from the stallion but when she came to the ridges of the corduroy road, she had to learn to step on the slippery planks.

Hours of riding brought them once more to the Ohio.

"How good it is to see the river again," Ann spoke with homesickness in her voice.

As they waited at the landing of the ferry that would carry them across to Wheeling, they watched keelboats poled with the current and long barges loaded with coal from Pittsburgh rowed by crews of sturdy men at the oars.

"I never knew the Ohio was such a busy river."

"All the way to New Orleans, too, after she joins up with the Mississippi. But it's tougher going up the river. A successful steamboat could revolutionize river traffic."

When the Wheeling ferry arrived, it was so loaded with a family of settlers and their household goods that the flat-bottomed boat set only inches from the water level.

The settler called out for anyone who would listen. "We be bound fer Maysville. It cost fifty cents to carry my wagon. I reckon the danged river's too wide fer a bridge, but I got me a passel o' kids they let come fer free."

The ferryboat was shaped the same at both ends, so it was possible to re-load it promptly for the return trip without waiting to be turned about.

The ferryman greeted each passenger to collect the charges. "Howdy-do, Colonel Zane, Sir, I reckon you be ridin' free seein' ez how you be the owner o' this here ferry."

Col. Zane turned to let other passengers load. "Why, Jonathan Jennings. Howdy there, Sir! I hear you're a Congressman now. Be you going to Washington City thisaway?"

"If it isn't Ebenezer Zane himself. We've just come from riding your Trace," introducing his wife. "I've been telling her that if you'd bring it all the way to Indiana, we'd have statehood in no time."

Jonathan turned to lead the horses on to the ferry but the ferryman stopped him. "I get twelve and a half cents fer the horses each but we be mighty full this trip. Can't they swim the river?"

Two families plus their possessions and live stock already filled the ferry to capacity. "The River's too wide for the mare," Jonathan replied. "I'll have to take her aboard but the stallion can follow the ferry at the end of the tow rope."

The ferryman blew a blast on his bull horn and prepared to pole away from the shore. Just as the negro rowers leaned on the great oars, a man with a bandaged head came swaggering to the landing, clutching a jug of whiskey. He lifted the jug for another draft when he suddenly realized that the ferryboat was pulling away from the dock.

The man staggered forward and made a clumsy leap over the widening gap of water. He barely managed to fall on the deck crashing into squealing pigs and a bawling cow.

At the far side of the boat, Ginger was skittish at the crowding of people and animals. Suddenly the little mare tensed. Her nostrils twitched and her ears pricked forward. She raised her head and pawed her forelegs savagely until it seemed she would make a hole in the floor boards.

"Whatever can be the trouble with Ginger?" Ann tightened her hold on the mare's reins. "We'll soon be across on land again, Ginger."

But suddenly, the mare ripped the reins from the startled Ann. With a fierce shriek that even Big Brown heard as he swam at the end of the tow rope, the mare stomped savagely and pulled free. She plunged through the passengers and animals and bolted across the ferry.

Ginger made straight for the man with the jug. She raised her forelegs and brought them down on the man's shoulders. Stunned, the surprised man somehow kept his feet. Still clinging to his jug, he staggered backwards against the very end of the boat.

Once again the angry mare raised her strong legs and with the full strength of her shoulder muscles, she pushed against the startled man until he fell backwards into the waters of the Ohio.

By this time the ferry had slipped into the current and the man sank deep. Ginger was poised to jump in after the man when Jonathan caught her reins and Col. Zane rushed to assist him. It took the full strength of the two men to hold the mare.

In seconds, the riverman re-appeared at the surface of the water still holding his jug, spluttering and thrashing about as he struggled to stay afloat. Shaking the water from his still bandaged head, he looked into the blazing red eyes of a snorting stallion. Big Brown was swimming toward him as close as the tow rope would permit.

The drunken riverman sobered fast. He let go of the jug and began to swim frantically away from the plunging stallion.

On the ferryboat all was confusion. Passengers were trying to calm the animals and Ann was trying to calm the passengers. Through all the turbulence, the stout rowers worked hard to keep the boat from swamping. When Big Brown had reached the full stretch of the tow rope, the horse pulled so hard, the boat began to spin out of control.

"That drunken bully was Evel Earthquake, the bragginest, fightinest brawler on the River. Evel's one riotin' riverman always lookin' for a fight but this is one he didn't win," and Col. Zane laughed heartily.

"Will he drown?" worried gentle Ann.

"Ol Evel Earthquake drown? He kin swim his way upstream to Pittsburgh."

"O dear, Pittsburgh is where we're going, isn't it, Jonathan? Do you think he'll be swimming to Pittsburgh?"

Col. Zane laughed. "Twas a comical sight. He sure sobered up fast, didn't he now? But Ma'am, whatever got into your mare to make her behave like that?"

He listened to their story. "We'll not be taking Evel on this ferry ever again, you may be sure o' that. If he wants to cross the Ohio, he kin swim with the horses."

Evel Earthquake was swimming the Ohio now, but he swam down the River with the current. Soon all that could be seen was the riverman's jug floating and bobbing on the surface of the River.

In spite of the chaos, the rowers had handled the side oars well and now the ferry was at last nearing the Wheeling shores. They had used the long steering oar at the stern to make allowances for the current at the ferry dock.

Streets fanned out from the River with brick and log houses and all kinds of trading centers. There was a sign for a blacksmith, a wheelwright, and a tannery—even for a hotel.

"Wheeling marks the end of my short-cut trace," said Zane.

"Senator Clay and I would like to see the federal government connect your Trace from Washington City and take it all the way to the Mississippi River. We go now to Canonsburg."

Col. Zane bid them Godspeed. "Mebbe you'll be seein' the first steamboat headin' down for the Mississippi. 'Fulton's Folly' folks be callin' it."

"I understand Nicholas Roosevelt's building it and he's plenty knowledgeable when it comes to boat building and river travel. I heard that he took his bride along on his first keelboat voyage to study the Big River."

"Wal, I 'spect folks'll be stickin' to my Trace awhile yet. I ain't seen a steamboat but it ain't likely to get launched even, much less be navigatin' the treacherous channels of the Mississip'. I'd soon take my chances on dry land with mountain bears."

Jonathan laughed. "I'll keep trying for a road then."

Soon on their way, Ann was full of questions. What had Col. Zane said about bears in the mountains? What was a steamboat like? Who was the bride who made a honeymoon voyage on the Big River? How soon would she be meeting her new kinfolk? Would they truly think Ann a suitable wife for their congressman-son?

IX

Steamboat Sendoff

The new trail followed high cliffs beside the Ohio River on its upward course to meet the Monongahela and the Allegheny Rivers in a triangle. Against the rolling hills on the far shore, the sun played patterns of shine and shadow.

"The Dufours were right in calling it 'La Belle Riviere'," explained Ann as they stopped to rest the horses.

They sat close with their backs against the wide trunk of a buckeye tree and watched the sparkling waters of the River rushing on its long way to New Orleans.

"We'll be leaving it soon. We'll be crossing the Youghiegheny and the Monongahela Rivers."

"Such beautiful names!"

"Indian names—Youghiegheny is river-that-flows-a-round-about-course. It's a tributary of the Monongahela—the river-of-the-skidding-banks. When heavy rains rampage the rivers, whole islands are sometimes swallowed up and disappear. Well, we've dallied long. There's yet a half-day's travel before sundown."

They slept that night in a friendly cabin. Ed Rhys and his wife would accept no payment for their generous hospitality.

"We like the company. It gets lonely here for my Carrie."

"Here's a buckeye-nut for luck then, for the big family you be wanting. Indians say it brings good fortune if you keep it polished."

The early sun was still flooding pink light against the soft clouds of the sky when they left the Rhys' cabin. Several hours of pastoral trails brought them in sight of a picturesque village set in a green valley. They came to pleasant streets where large shade trees sheltered an occasional house. Before Ann realized what was happening, Jonathan was cantering down a lane that led to a square red-bricked house set back from the road. A carriage stood before the house with a team of horses hitched and waiting.

"Here we are!" Jonathan shouted triumphantly.

At the sound of the riders, a lady came to the door. She was dressed for travelling with a veil tying down her hat.

"Mother! I've come with my bride!" Jonathan shouted in a voice like a barker's at a carnival. Before Ann could straighten her

99

skirt or pin straggling locks of hair, the lady was hurrying down the steps to meet them.

"It's Jonathan, it's Jonathan!" she called back. Almost at once, Ann was engulfed in embrace after embrace. "This is my mother, my father, my sister, my brothers, my aunt, my cousins. ." Jonathan introduced breathlessly, his face flushed with pride.

"So you're the girl who married my spoiled brother!"

"Shame, Sister, you'll frighten our new daughter before she can get to know us," spoke the mother with gentleness. "This is Jonathan's sister Ann—now we have two Ann's."

"Bless you, dear daughter. This is a happy day," and it was Reverend Jennings' turn to kiss the bride.

Brother Obadiah clapped Jonathan on the back. "We never thought you'd get yourself such a beauty, you old bachelor, you!"

Jonathan was suddenly concerned. "You're dressed for travel and the horses are standing?"

All began to explain at once. "We're riding to Pittsburgh to witness the launching of the *New Orleans*. It's the first steamboat to brave the Mississippi River."

"You're just in time. Commodore Roosevelt and Madame Lydia have invited us to come aboard to see their living quarters for the voyage."

"It's a dangerous adventure our friends are embarking on."

"Wait till you hear our adventures," but there was no time for that now. Ann was welcomed into the pleasant home where they were quickly refreshed and made ready to join the spectators of the steamboat's much heralded departure.

"Grandma's keeping the children. She's sure the steamboat will explode and she didn't want to be around to see it fly apart."

"Grandma doesn't take to such new-fangled ideas that are again Nature," and they all laughed.

It was arranged that Ann would ride in the carriage with the ladies with Reverend Jennings to handle the reins. The men would follow on horseback.

"What about Ginger?" Ann asked timidly, already seated in the carriage with the ladies.

"We'll leave her in the stables for a day of rest." But as Jonathan started to lead her away, the little mare became aware she was being left behind in this strange place. Like a spoiled child, Ginger pulled back and snorted in a whimpering fuss.

Ann jumped down from the carriage in a most unladylike manner and went directly to her mare. "Look, Jonathan, Ginger's afraid. She might be stolen again."

Obadiah laughed. "Horse stealing's a mighty serious offense in Pennsylvania. It's not likely in these parts."

"But I saw a sheriff's broadside warning of a horse thief in this very area," Ann persisted. "Jonathan, I am going to ride Ginger." Ann spoke firmly, used to getting her way.

"Ann, do as I say." Jonathan was stern. "Get back into the carriage at once. Ginger stays."

Ann looked at her husband in amazement. She knew she had promised in her marriage vows to "obey." Is this what it meant? She felt her blood warm in anger and embarrassment. Her eyes flashed. Ugly words rose to her lips, but before she could speak, Jonathan's sternness vanished.

"All right, confound it! I'll lead Ginger beside Big Brown, but you ride in the carriage to become acquainted." Then he added, "The mare probably needs new shoes anyhow, and we'll be stopping at the blacksmith's."

Was this Jonathan's way of saving face before his family, for he was aware how perfect a Morgan horse like Ginger holds shoes to the last? All were watching and Ann dropped her head in shame.

But she got obediently into the carriage and Ginger snorted in approval as she trotted at the stallion's side. Ann tried to explain her fears for the mare and told the story of her kidnapping.

"No wonder you were anxious," Sister Ann spoke sympathetically. "Why didn't Jonathan explain?"

Jonathan's mother intervened. "Command and obey in a marriage is a two-way road and it comes from loving. When I watched you both compromise, I knew your marriage will go well."

"Amen, amen!" teased Sister Ann. "You sound like Paw."

Ann blushed but she joined in the friendly laughter. It was good to feel comfortable with her new family.

A festive air filled the carriage now. Skies were clear and the air was crisp with the spice of early autumn. Pleasant sounds of female chatter carried back to the men following on horseback. Jonathan was satisfied that all was cordial between Ann and his family, and when she waved to him, he knew that peace had been restored between them, too.

101

The road carried them past Jefferson Academy, where Reverend John McMillen had taught Latin and Greek to Jonathan and brother Obadiah to admit them to the new Washington College eight miles away.

"My brothers travelled the eight miles to the College every day. They had only one old horse between the two of them so they rode ride-and-tie."

"What do you mean 'ride-and-tie'?" Ann asked, eager to learn about her husband.

"It worked this way. Jonathan rode a piece and then he'd tie the old horse to a tree and begin walking. Obadiah walked till he came to the horse to take his riding turn. He rode a piece and then tied the horse again to wait for Jonathan, while Obadiah took another walking turn."

"They named their old nag *Professor Ride-n-Tie*," said the father and they all laughed together.

The road passed through rolling hills and valleys whose gentle sylvan beauty was in sharp contrast to the dark impenetrable forests of the wilderness. A short ferry ride took them, carriages, horses, and all, across the Monongahela River where the two rivers left a triangular point of land between.

Here the pastoral view yielded to the sight of factories and smoke as the town of Pittsburgh came into view. The sky held clouds of dust from the coal of furnaces and forges. Reverend Jennings pointed out the kilns where the bricks for their house had been fired. "And there's the Redstone Furnace Company that made our cookstove."

The mother pointed to one ugly building with few windows. "There's machinery in there that cards and spins and weaves. I've been sent for to doctor in some emergency and the working conditions are dreadful."

"You doctor?" Ann gasped.

Jonathan's mother laughed at her surprise. "I've had study of medicinal herbs."

"We doctor together," Reverend Jennings added. "I doctor souls while Mama doctors bodies."

The carriage bumped its way down a brick-laid street where signs declared wares and services for sale. An iron hat, broad brimmed as a Quaker's hung before the shop of the hatter and a large iron boot swung from a bracket before the shoemaker's.

When they came to a sign with a great iron horseshoe, they brought the horses to a stop.

"Here's Barney the blacksmith."

Just as they pulled up to dismount, a great pack of wild dogs rushed barking from the fields. They lunged snarling and growling at the legs of the horses. Ginger was terrorized. She snatched at her bit and swung her hind quarters wildly.

Jonathan and Obadiah dismounted and brandished their riding whips at the ugly pack, but the dogs continued to yip and snap at the horses. Ginger grew more and more agitated as the yelping dogs seemed to single out the riderless mare.

Suddenly Big Brown sounded terrifying screams of battle, pounding his forelegs like pistons. One by one, the dogs backed away from the stallion until finally the whole pack slinked off down the street.

Barney was already out of the smithy calming Ginger. "This one could be a Morgan horse from the looks of her and they don't cotton much to dogs. Got to be particular about rabies hereabouts. Dogs get the crazies. But I don't see no slobbers on this one."

He examined Ginger carefully lifting each hoof to his leather apron. "Every shoe on the little mare is tight and sound. I'll just be cleaning her hoofs, but the big stallion here—he could be a shoe-thrower. Leave the horses, Mister Jennings—or should I be saying Congressman Jennings, is it? Get along now all of you, to see the *New Orleans*. She's a boat as pretty as your bride here."

Ann blushed.

"Thank you, Barney. You've been doing right by our horses for many years—even old Professor Ride-n-Tie."

Everyone laughed and Ann felt a sense of belonging to her new family for she could share in the story of Jonathan's old horse.

The horses were left in the care of Barney. "The big stallion'll help," he laughed.

This time the little mare paid no notice as Ann joined the others eager to witness the send-off of a steamboat that was soon to challenge the great Mississippi River itself.

More people than Ann had ever imagined were heading toward the launching of the *New Orleans*.

"All Pittsburgh's five thousand population must be here," said Jonathan as he and Ann pushed their way along with the crowds.

For many weeks when folks came to market, they had watched the building of the steamboat. They had even witnessed work carried on at night by the light of torches to hasten completion of the boat before snowtime. Few had ever seen the Big River they had heard so many wild stories about, and most doubted that the *New Orleans* could ever reach it but no one wanted to miss today's history-making episode.

They knew Robert Fulton had sailed his new-fangled invention on the Hudson River in New York State. They had read in the Pittsburgh Gazette how the Governor of Louisiana Territory was so impressed by the new invention that he had ordered the building of the *New Orleans* to navigate the lower part of the Mississippi River. Young Nicholas Roosevelt had been brought all the way from New York to build the boat. Today the *New Orleans* would be on its way to be delivered to fulfill the order.

"He found plenty of boat builders here," Jonathan explained to Ann, "but Mister Roosevelt had to bring the materials for the boat's machinery all the way from New York and even the mechanics to put it together."

"Sister Ann told me that he brought his wife, too," Ann replied, "and she planned the elegant furnishings for the boat. I can hardly wait to see."

"Her father is Benjamin Latrobe, the great architect and designer. We'll be seeing his work in Washington."

Crowds were already lining the bluffs overlooking the riverbanks of the Monongahela. "O do let's hurry!" Ann clung to Jonathan almost dancing in anticipation.

Then they got their first view of the steamboat. There it lay at the foot of Boyd's Hill. No oars, no poles, no sails,—only great paddlewheels to churn the waters and two handsome cabins fore and aft with a gay-colored awning to shield passengers from the sun. Could such a strange boat really run the channels of the Great River?

Obadiah pointed out Beelen's Foundry on the mouth of the small creek. "That's where they put her together. They floated the white pine for her planking right into the shipyard."

"And they sure ran into plenty of problems," Cousin Joshua informed them. "The waters of the Monongahela backed up into the shipyards and set all the materials afloat. One day, the high waters set the whole boat afloat."

104

To reach the steamboat, the family must clamber down the steep bluffs to the landing. They were welcomed aboard by Commodore Roosevelt with his young wife, Lydia. Madame Roosevelt was a lady, but like Ann, she was ready to risk discomforts and dangers to be at the side of her husband in his adventures.

"We are to be the only passengers," said Commodore Roosevelt as he and his wife escorted the visitors over the boat, "but we have a full-sized staff to operate her and look after us."

"It is hard to believe that after all our difficulties," added Lydia, "we are ready at last to take the *New Orleans* on her maiden voyage."

Captain Jack was the first of the crew to greet the visitors. "I was strictly a flat-boat man before I succumbed to Nicholas Roosevelt's persuasiveness. The *Orleans*, she's one fine boat."

"Sir, why do you call the boat *she*?" Ann asked timidly.

"Cause she's as beautiful as a lady, Ma'am," Captain Jack answered, gallantly bowing to the ladies.

Jonathan sought out the engineer. "Why does the *Orleans* carry two masts fore and aft?"

"When the wind is favorable, Sir, sails can boost her speed but she'll make her way under her own steam fast enough. The *New Orleans* can pass a piece of wood floatin' on the River as fast as you could pass on land with your trotting horses."

There was no sign of the mysterious machinery hidden below deck. "What of the capricious channels of the Mississippi and the dangers of shoals and sandbars?" Obadiah asked the pilot, who was respected as the best and longest-experienced pilot on the Big River. "I understand there are no charts for the navigation."

"Only those Master Roosevelt spelled out on his keelboat voyage. I've niver piloted a steamboat on the Mississip' and I sure niver piloted a boat what cost $38,000, but I'm bettin' on this here boat," and he left them to climb the ladder to the pilot house, setting like a box on top of the spacious cabin.

Six deckhands, two servants, a waiter, and a cook, plus one huge Newfoundland dog, completed the party aboard the boat.

"You call him *Tiger*?" Ann looked at the slow moving dog in surprise. "He stands almost as high as my mare."

"Don't let his name mislead you," Lydia laughed.

While the men went below to view the machinery, Lydia led the ladies to the cabin quarters. They were not only surprised at the size of the steamboat but they were even more astonished to see the family cabins.

Furnishings were more beautiful and complete than Ann recalled from homes she had visited in Kentucky. Cabinets held delicate china and monogrammed silver. The galley where food was prepared was so tiny the plump cook filled it till there was no space for visitors. Just outside on the deck was a masonry fireplace also used for cooking.

"Will you be afraid of the river travel?" Ann asked one of the maids.

"Yes, Mum, begging the lady's pardon. Folk say there be monsters in the River we be goin' on." She raised her eyes to the heavens and made the sign of the cross like a prayer.

"Bridget is bound to us in servitude," Lydia explained.

"I thought the state of New York did not hold with slavery."

"We don't own Bridget like property. She is indentured to work for us until she has earned the passage money from her old country, which we paid."

"If I be so bold, Mum," Bridget interjected, "It's a lucky girl I am, God bless 'em—even if I be fearful."

As the others moved on, Lydia invited Ann to sit with her under the awning. "I hear you are on a honeymoon-journey, Madame Jennings. It must have been frightening riding through the wilderness."

"We had some dangerous times but I fear little when I can be with my husband." Ann spoke briefly then of their adventures. "But what of you, Madame Roosevelt? I've been told that your honeymoon-journey was a river voyage."

"It was a journey on a flatboat, actually to prepare for this voyage. It was my first river trip, but Mister Roosevelt thought of my every comfort. He even designed a bridal suite."

"A bridal suite on a flatboat?" The two ladies giggled together like girls instead of dignified married ladies.

"We floated all the way down to New Orleans but my husband kept so busy recording channels and river currents, he had little time to attend me," and Lydia sighed at the recollection.

"I understand there are those who think you should not be making this trip, Madame Roosevelt—that it is too dangerous."

Lydia laughed. "Yes, some think my Nicholas is a monster for taking me along, especially since I am to become a mother, but I assure you, I, too, am much braver with my husband than without him. Besides, boats are my Nicholas' way of life and I like the sharing."

Ann nodded in agreement. "Government is important to my husband and I find it well to be learning the needs of my country."

The companionable visit came to an abrupt end when they began to feel the vibrations of machinery. A whistle screamed, powered by clouds of steam belching from the smoke stack.

Lydia and Ann moved quickly to join the others. Here they found great commotion and bustle. In the midst of the confusion, Reverend Jennings raised his hand for quiet. In a voice that even people lining the bluffs above could hear, he began to pray.

"We ask God's blessings upon the *New Orleans* on its maiden voyage, and on all those on boat or shore who have a part in its destined purpose. Amen!"

A great hush fell as the crowds waited for the final fanfare— the firing of a canon required for every boat on leaving the port.

Children giggled nervously and put their hands to their ears as they waited. Adults stood quietly, heads bowed as if still in prayer. Then a great boom sounded and a discharge of smoke filled the air. From the hills across the River, hundreds of carrier pigeons rose in flight. Babies cried and parents laughed uneasily. Echos from the boom grew fainter and fainter as they faded in final farewells across the waters.

"All ashore that's going ashore!" came the last cry. It was time to wish Godspeed to the Roosevelts.

Ann spoke her thanks to Lydia and then recollected the letter she had written at the Rhys' cabin. "I'd be most grateful to you, Madame Roosevelt, if you would carry my letter to Indiana. When you reach Louisville, it could be sent by carrier on to Charles Town."

"I see you have faith in the success of our voyage, Madame Jennings. If we're to be wrecked, I promise to see that your letter doesn't drown with the boat," and Lydia laughed gaily.

Obadiah was reluctant to disembark. "This steamboat could sure beat old Professor Ride-n-Tie."

Barges and keelboats pulled close now with their crews curious to view the strange boat. Lusty voices sang as they rowed in rhythm:

> The river is up, the channel is deep,
> The winds blow high and strong.
> The flash of the oars, the stroke we keep,
> As we row the old boat along.

"The rivermen are a swaggering, gambling lot but they are warm comrades," Obadiah commented.

"I don't wish anything to do with rivermen," Ann spoke with vehemence. "That one looks like Evel Earthquake," pointing to a robust rower. "O Jonathan, could it be?"

Jonathan laughed. "Even Evel Earthquake couldn't swim up river that fast."

To get a closer view, one crew bushwacked their boat along the shore by pulling from one overhanging branch to another. "Some rows up, but we rows down, all the way to Shawneetown; Pullaway, pullaway!" sang the crew.

Some taunted the crew of the *New Orleans*: "She's a rich man's folly!" they called out. "She'll never make it—put her on a barge and we'll take her along," they bellowed.

The happy holiday crowd cheered the river crews. Suddenly the ear-jarring blast of a horn screeched from the steamboat.

Reverend Jennings laughed. "That should bring good luck for it must have scared away the devil himself."

Full attention was now directed to the steamboat. Her crew had untied the heavy rope that held her to the landing dock and clouds of smoke and steam rose from her lofty stacks. The two great paddlewheels slowly began to turn. Puffing and wheezing, the *New Orleans* began to move.

When the crowd realized that the steamboat was actually heading out, shout after shout ripped through the crowd. "Hip, hip, hooray! Hip, hip, hooray!" Men threw their hats into the air and women waved white handkerchiefs with cries of Godspeed. Again and again the crew of the steamboat returned the crowd's cheers.

"It's not for believing," said one onlooker. "No poles, no oars, no sails! She sounds like she's explodin'."

"A spark-spittin' monster she is, a settin' too deep in the water. She's gonna sink, I tell ya," cried another.

As the space of water between boat and land slowly widened, the steamboat headed majestically upstream. Then she made a full circuit and with a puff of steam and the blast of her horn, the boat moved into her proper course. The *New Orleans* was pointed down the Ohio on her long way over two thousand miles of turbulent, uncharted waters, to the city for which she was named.

"Take a last look there, Son," one father said to his boy. "She'll never make it back."

"We'll be a missin' her a buildin' on Boyd's Hill."

"Dangerous sailing ahead—shifting channels, no charts— they must be daft."

"I ain't niver seen this Big River they talk about, but I been hearing talk of river pirates and Indians attackin' in canoes."

One of the ladies was dabbing her eyes. "Whatever does her husband mean imperiling Lydia Roosevelt's life this way?" Then she lowered her voice, "Did you know that Madame Roosevelt is going to be a mother?"

"Well, I never! It's downright scandalous her going off like that."

But on the deck of the *New Orleans*, Lydia Roosevelt stood serene and smiling at Nicholas' side. "What a brave lady!" Ann said to Jonathan.

"Like you, my dear."

The steamboat began to disappear beyond the headlands on the right banks of the Ohio. The hissing engines sounded through the air and the plunge of the paddlewheels caught the water in splash and sparkle. Some ran along the bluffs for a last glimpse of the *New Orleans* and its courageous passengers.

The River was busy with the traffic of keelboats and barges but they seemed strangely quiet after the hissing and rumbling engines of the steamboat.

On shore, the scene changed into a holiday fair to celebrate the successful launching of the strange new boat. Entertainers mixed through the crowds. A troupe of jugglers tossed hoops and plates high into the air and minstrel singers strolled with banjos and fiddles.

A monkey on a chain jumped to music ground out of a box. With a little red cap over one eye, the monkey turned somersaults and passed his cap for coins. When the monkey jumped on Ann's shoulder, she was delighted and Jonathan threw some fips into his little cap.

"Come on, Ann, I'm hungry."

Stalls' had been set up everywhere with exciting array of food and liquids. "I'd like to sample every one."

Jonathan was doing just that. He had piled his plate with juicy-looking pot pie beside dumplings and doughballs, and a great helping of pickled pig's feet and smokehouse meats.

"Don't mind Jonathan," called Sister Ann. "Try this Schnitz and Gnepp—it's a German way of cooking dumplings in ham broth with dried apples."

"What do you call it?"

Sister laughed at her confusion. "Our state of Pennsylvania has the best cooks in the world. Early settlers came here from the Rhineland and the hausfraus brought recipes with them. Here— try some Speck and Bono. It's Jonathan's favorite—green beans cooked with ham and potatoes."

"Have a piece of shoo-fly pie," as the Mother gave Ann a circular-shaped pie, warm and spicy. "Fried pies are for dunking," she said.

"Yah!" came from a jolly hausfrau. "Eat till it ouches you."

"Our journey home is better made before the sun is outened," reminded a Dutch cousin, "and the day is fast closing out."

With reluctance they left the merrymaking behind and returned to their carriage. The horses had been turned into green pasturing and Ginger was fully recovered from her encounter with the dogs. "I'm happy Ginger didn't meet up with the Roosevelt's Tiger," laughed Ann.

The ride home was filled with chatter and talk of the events of the day. Jonathan had once sent a letter to his family telling of his coming marriage to Ann Gilmore Hay: "I have chosen a woman of great goodness of disposition, of common sense—a lady enough for me—a *very* woman."*

---

* From Jonathan Jennings' letter to his Sister Ann, courtesy of the Indiana Historical Society.

His family had marvelled when this beautiful young girl braved the hardships and dangers of the journey to accompany Jonathan the long way to Washington. Now they, too, had found that Ann was truly "a *very* woman."

That night Jonathan and Ann lay together in the great feather bed of the guest room.

"It's been another wondrous beginning day, Jonathan. I never knew there could be so many."

But Jonathan was already asleep with his arms about her.

X

Crossing The Alleghenys

A day of easy riding brought them to tree-lined bluffs above
the Monongahela River which divided the village of Brownsville
into two towns. On one side they found boat builders and saw-
mills and Ann counted eighteen stores.

On the other side, they began to climb Grips Knob where
they could see enchanting country of knobs and hills, always
drawing them closer to the mountains.

They met a Conestoga wagon pulled by a team of six sturdy
horses carrying settlers heading west with children, parents, and
assorted relatives. The sides and wheels of the great wagon were
painted bright red with blue running gear. The bridles of the lead
horses were fancied up with red rosettes and ribbons.

Ann spoke into Ginger's ear, "How'd you like some rosettes
now that you've lost your chapeau?" To the driver she asked, "Do
not wagon horses wear bells to let folks know the wagon is
approaching?"

"You're right, Ma'am, and we be missin' the sound o' 'em."

"And folks comin' to wave us past," added his wife, "but we
done lost 'em."

"You mean they were stolen?"

"You see, Ma'am," the driver explained, "it's the way of the
road fer wagon drivers to stop and help if there be trouble. I had
me the misfortune of gittin' into a hole a ways back, and the
wagonner who helped me, 'twas his right to take my bells for his
trouble."

"But we aim to git 'em back," said the wife.

"Yep, the next time I find a driver in a spit o' trouble, I git his
bells, and on this trail, I be sure as sartain to find wagonners a
needin' help."

"Your horses look powerful enough, but how do you get
your wagon over the mountains?" queried Jonathan.

"Onct we had to unload her and let 'er down with a block and
tackle."

"Is there no faster way?" worried Ann.

"Like fallin' down, mebbe. Of course, you could fly with an
eagle a comin' this way if you could catch a ride." Pleased at his

own humour, the wagonner slapped his thigh with a hearty laugh and his woman folk joined in.

The great Conestoga moved out, with its canvas top swelling like the sail of a ship. "I'm learning much about my country's courageous people," Ann spoke thoughtfully as they went on their own way.

That night they stayed in Peter Colley's Tavern. Colley had first opened his own cabin for overnight guests back in 1796 and had grown rich off the travellers. But he produced privacy for sleeping and a chamberpot under the bed to save guests the need for a cold run outdoors in the night. Their bed held only a straw-tick mattress that rustled and itched but "At least we don't have to share the mattress with strangers," Ann exclaimed.

Ann accepted the situation with her usual good grace. As they set forth the next morning, Ann studied the view checkered with patterns of forest and farmland, and steep hills dotted with slits of coal chambers. "Are the mountains close now?"

"Only the foothills. You could see the mountains if it weren't for this early autumn haze, but they're still thirty miles away."

They lost no time in trotting the horses across the last remaining valley and that night they stayed at Uniontown where they met other travellers. Some were preparing for the formidable climb up Laurel Hill, while others arrived from the East exhausted from their days of rugged travel.

"Don't be alarmed, Ann," as they listened to travel-talk. "We'll be finding the trail easier riding our good horses."

The next morning they commenced the long journey through the Alleghenys. By late afternoon, the horses were struggling to maintain their footing along the continuous steep ascent, a thousand feet straight up Laurel Hill. It was colder in the mountains and for the first time, Ann pulled her cloak warm about her and its hood over her head. Breath rose from the horses in foggy puffs of vapor.

"Winter comes early in the mountains, doesn't it?" Ann commented.

"We'll be meeting travellers trying to beat the winter blizzards."

But now they began the descent. They trod descending slopes so slanted that Ginger's head lay below Ann's feet and her body kept pushing against the front pommel of her saddle. "I feel as if I'm falling off the mountain, head over heels."

At first Ginger slipped in the mud left by almost daily mountain showers, but the spunky little mare soon learned to sidle her way down the steep trail. As Ann clung to the pommels of her sidesaddle, she found that to see ahead, she had to look over her own shoulder.

Jonathan was full of respect for both horses. Big Brown was no surprise for he and Jonathan had travelled the mountains together before. But he was full of admiration for the little mare, who until this journey, had climbed only the gentle hills of southern Indiana.

"Your horse is like you, Ann. You both show courage and endurance." Then he patted the taut neck of Big Brown straining to hold back on a steep decline. "The wilderness couldn't be settled without horses."

"Or without women!"

Jonathan laughed. "That's right. You're both good stayers—horses and women."

They were riding over a small hillock just then and they saw a wagon ahead bumping its rough way downgrade. A small caravan of men, women, and children were following on foot, when suddenly the wagon struck a boulder and began to tip crazily to its side.

Jonathan and Ann reined their horses as the wagon over-turned with a crash that echoed through the mountainside. They quickly dismounted and ran to the scene. The overturned wagon had come to rest against a sturdy chestnut tree. The lone horse was sitting on his haunches with the shaft and reins in a tangled confusion.

There was a frenzy of shouting and yelling. Women screamed and babies cried. The vehicle's contents were scattered across the steep hillside.

"Is anyone hurt?" Jonathan called out but the answers came in a jumble of gestures and rolling eyes and in the words of some foreign language.

The people were dressed in garish-colored shirts and skirts, with flashy head scarves over black hair that hung about swarthy-skinned faces.

"They look strange—shouldn't we ride fast by?"

The men stood helpless. The wheels of the wagon were unbroken but the lean old nag made no attempt to stand.

Jonathan knew he had no obligation to stay but how could he leave these poor people in such distress. "Tie the horses, Ann, and hold my rifle. I'll see what can be done."

Using signs and gestures, Jonathan began to restore order. First, they pulled the frightened, struggling horse to its four feet. With grunting and groaning, the men heaved the wagon back on its wheels and began to pull it back up the trail.

Ann set Jonathan's rifle aside, to try to help, too. She quieted a crying baby and helped the hysterical women collect the spilled possessions.

At long last, the wagon was re-loaded and order was restored. "We'll ride on now. Where is my gun, Ann?"

A look of terror crossed Ann's face. She rushed to the spot where she had carefully placed the rifle. It was not there.

Suddenly the whole crowd was blocking the way, shouting and gesturing, keeping them from the horses.

"Let us pass," commanded Jonathan, but the crowd stood solidly together. Suddenly the crowd parted to reveal a young boy holding fast to Jonathan's gun. With much pointing and gesturing, some of the men thrust the boy forward. He stood hanging his head in shame. Then reluctantly, he held the gun outstretched in his two hands to Jonathan.

In hushed silence, Jonathan took his rifle from the boy. At the same moment, a beautiful dark-eyed girl stepped forward. Softly and slowly, the girl began to speak haltingly words of English.

"Boy bad. Not steal. You help us. We thank. We are entertainers with much travel. Now we entertain for you to thank."

From across the trail came the lilting sound of a violin, and the girl began to sing in a rich sultry voice, turning and swaying to the melody. As the fiddler played livelier and faster, others took up the song and the girl began to dance, spinning and twirling to match the ever-faster cadence. Now all began to clap, keeping time for the dancer who was as nimble as the fiddler's fingers and as graceful as his bowing.

The girl held her arms out to Ann and suddenly she found herself joining in the dance, turning and twirling, copying the girl's every movement as well as her heavy riding skirt would permit.

The women and children, too, began to turn and swing with the music, faster and faster, until their skirts flew out from their waists, spinning like the colors of a spiral top.

Abruptly it all came to an end as unexpectedly as it had begun. The children spun off from the dance and fell laughing to the ground. Ann took Jonathan's arm. She was breathless but her eyes still shone with the excitement of the dance.

The men bowed low to Jonathan and Ann. As they turned once again to mount their patient horses, a very old woman shuffled forward and stood boldly blocking Ann's way. Jonathan was annoyed at another delay. This time he held his rifle ready.

Once more the dancing girl tried to explain, "Old woman like you. She tell fortune."

"My fortune? How exciting! O please do let her, Jonathan. I've never had my fortune told."

The woman already held Ann's hand in a claw-like vise. With gnarled fingers, she traced the lines in Ann's palms.

"What does she see?" Ann asked the dancing girl.

"She see many things. Happiness with your Mister. He gentleman—important man."

Jonathan looked pleased. "Ask her when Indiana will get statehood. Maybe she sees that I could be the first governor."

But the fortune teller ignored him. "You travel far, Lady," the black-eyed girl translated. "You be good for people where you go. Maybe trouble a little."

"What kind of trouble? In Washington?"

The dancer shrugged. "She say no worry."

Jonathan was impatient. "Come—this is nonsense—we must be on our way." Then seeing Ann's disturbed expression, he spoke more gently. "Here—give her this," handing Ann a silver shin. "We'd best hurry on."

But when Ann tried to give the piece of silver to the old woman, she shook her head. Once again the dancing girl spoke for her. "She say she old woman. She no fiddle. No dance. Make you good fortune. She thank you."

With those words, the dancing girl took from her ears two round golden hoops the size of Ann's little wrists, and to Ann's surprise, she placed them into her hands. "For you!"

117

Ann curtsied. Then she turned and kissed the old woman's furrowed cheek. She knew that a kiss has its own language and would need no translation.

As the two rode off down the mountain trail, no one tried to stop them this time. But the lingering melody of a fiddle seemed to follow them as if it were suspended in some mountain echo.

As they made their way through the Alleghenys, the riders were forced to tunnel through pockets of fog and walk the horses through cold mountain streams. Before starting up the formidable Keyser Ridge they stayed the night in Harmony House, an old stone tavern in the village called Geneva.

"This is the village of Albert Gallatin who came here from another Geneva in Switzerland and founded a glass works."

"Do they make window-glass for their cabins," asked Ann, "instead of using your letters?"

Jonathan laughed. "You catch on fast but Gallatin's beautiful house is called Friendship Hill and you may be sure it is no cabin. Albert Gallatin is Secretary of the Treasury—a mighty important man in Washington City."

"O Jonathan, what will it be like for me in Washington City? I'll be fearful meeting such distinguished people."

"Now, Ann, you were reluctant to meet my family, remember? I shall be very proud to present my beautiful bride."

"And I'll be proud of my congressman-husband."

"Don't be forgetting that I'll be only one of many—and only a delegate-congressman from a Territory not even yet a state," and Jonathan sighed.

Keyser Ridge proved less awesome than Ann anticipated, for up the two monstrous hills, the trail followed an easy zig-zag course. But on descending the mountain, they came to a narrow pass in a deep-rutted ravine, where a rocky incline blocked the view of the trail ahead.

Suddenly the shrill blast of a horn shattered the mountain stillness. The sound was so close it caused both horses to rear. Before Ann knew what was happening, she had slid from her saddle and went tumbling down a rugged slope. She came to rest against a prickly bush, almost at the feet of a robust wagonner.

"I blowed the horn to warn you the wagon was comin', you tarned idiot."

"By hokey, it's a girl!" his fellow driver shouted. "What in tarnation is a dad-blasted girl doin' ridin' the mountains?"

"And a ridin' sidesaddle," spoke the first man seeing Ginger standing with her reins tangled on a bush and hanging her head in shame to have tossed her mistress. "What ya think you be—a confounded *lady*?"

Jonathan was quickly at her side, but Ann had already scrambled to her feet. "I'm all right, Jonathan," as she felt her bruises and scratches.

She was unhurt but she was angry to be seen sprawled before the men with her pantaloons showing and her hair tumbling down her back. Then she saw that Jonathan was ready to fight the men for their rudeness.

Ann quickly re-mounted Ginger. "Come, Mister Jennings, let's ride past them."

But once beyond sight and sound of the wagon, Ann let out a groan.

"What's the matter? Are you hurt after all?"

She cried tearfully, "I'm sitting on burrs. I fell against a prickly bush."

Slowly and painfully dismounting, Ann tried to hide behind a clump of bushes. With skirts hoisted above her waist, she began to pull off cockleburrs that clung to her pantaloons like leeches to a dog. There seemed to be hundreds of the sharp stickers.

Jonathan began to laugh. "I've heard of bats-in-the-belfry," he snickered as he tried to help Ann, "but bless me, if I ever heard of burrs-in-the-britches."

He sobered at once when he saw Ann turn stoney-faced with anger. She let him help her mount the mare to sit carefully into her saddle but she spoke no word.

They were well past the encounter with the wagonners when Big Brown began to falter, often standing with his mighty head drooping even when Jonathan urged him forward.

"What's the matter with Big Brown?" Ann's irritation with Jonathan forgotten in her concern for the horse.

"He's walking lame. We should be coming soon to Grantsville. It's a fair-sized village and I'll seek the smithy there."

"What if he can't be ridden?"

"I expect I'd have to leave him behind and hire a post horse for the rest of the journey."

Ginger turned sad eyes toward Big Brown as if she understood Jonathan's words.

Ann recalled the words of Barney the Blacksmith back in Pittsburgh. "You got to be particular about rabies hereabouts," he had said. What if Big Brown had rabies from the slobbers of the wild dogs! "Please God, no," she prayed. But she spoke none of this to Jonathan.

When they reached the village, Jonathan tied Ginger to the horse-rail before Castleman House and led the sick-acting Big Brown to the nearby blacksmith's. Ann was left to enter the tavern to wait alone in the Commons Room.

Grantsville was situated between two mountains in the center of the coal basin so it was a popular stopping place. The Commons Room proved to be a bar, a postoffice, a store, and a gathering place for wagonners after rugged mountain journeys.

When Ann entered, the room was full, but she was the only lady present. She took a seat on a bench and sat alone and dejected when she suddenly became aware that a man at the bar was staring. She turned away quickly but the man came to the bench and pushed himself beside her.

"Be ye a drinkin' one, woman?" he spoke in friendly fashion.

Before she could move, the landlord was at her side, and the man quickly moved away.

"He won't bother you further, Lady. I'll vouch for that. Wagonners are a hard-drinking, hard swearing lot, but they like a bit of the comradeship now and again. Come, there's another room."

Ann followed the landlord when suddenly, he stopped. "Here's the doctor now."

"The doctor?" Ann was puzzled. Could it be the horse-doctor with bad news of Big Brown?

An elderly man entered carrying a doctor's well-worn bag. He moved briskly to a far corner where a young boy was lying on a corn-husk mattress on the floor. When he saw the doctor, the boy groaned.

The doctor looked around and seeing the only woman present he said to Ann, "Here, Lady, hold this basin. I'll have to vomit the lad."

Taken completely by surprise, Ann hesitated. "Don't be afraid, Lady—he's just got the bilious-colic."

Ann held the pan. When the doctor completed his treatment, he left as abruptly as he had come with never a thank-you for Ann's assistance. She was annoyed at his rudeness, but she knew that doctors regarded caring for the sick to be a woman's rightful privilege.

Ann sought cold water to bathe the boy's forehead and he fell asleep. To herself she prayed that whatever was wrong with Big Brown would be cured as quickly.

No one took notice of her now as she moved back to the bench, for folks were gathered about a newly-arrived circuit riding preacher, who was shouting in a voice to fill the room. The men at the bar listened as they emptied their mugs, interrupting often to call to some new arrival. Word had got about the village, for women, too, had come now to hear the preacher urge his listeners to beware of sin.

There were interruptions from the cries of a peddler who had spread out his wares before the gathered crowd. A lawyer came shouting for a client he was seeking. All was noise and activity yet the preacher kept on.

At last, Ann saw Jonathan push through the crowded room. "O what is it, Jonathan? Does Big Brown have rabies?"

"Is that what you have been thinking? Poor Ann. The stallion's all right. His shoe caught one of the stickers from the burr bush, too. He'll be sore enough so we'll wait till morning to start up Chestnut Ridge."

Ann hugged her husband in relief but no one even noticed. "Where can we stay the night then?"

"I've obtained sleeping arrangements here, but the land-lord's charges are excessive. It will cost me double my travel allowance for bed and breakfast and stabling."

"Goodness, is there no other place?"

"He's got the only place in the valley. Some landlords take advantage when they know travellers can't stay long enough to bring suit for overcharging."

The Inn had two cabins joined by a passageway where travellers could find a basin and pitcher of water and a roller towel. Ann washed her hands but she scorned the dirty towel on its roller and dried them with her handkerchief.

"At least the board is good," Jonathan said as the landlord set before them ample amounts of "fish, flesh and fowl" as he promised, plus bread and eggs. They ate at a long table with a continuous smacking and slurping from fellow diners. Across the room, the preacher droned on.

All at once, a raucous shriek roared from the mountain-side. The preacher was quickly forgotten as everyone rushed for the door.

"Is it Indians?" Ann was alarmed.

"It's ride-for-the-bottle, folks," explained the landlord. "There's gonna be a weddin'. There's always a weddin' when word gets to the mountains that a preacher's come to town."

"Yahoo! Yaah-hooo!"

"Here they come—riders for the bottle."

From down the steep mountain-side, two riders raced headlong through brush and rocks to reach the bride waiting at her cabin door. The riders jumped their horses over logs and muddy holes each vying to be the first to reach her.

It was a close race. When the first rider reached the bride, the second was already half off his horse. Amidst the cheers of the crowd, the bride presented the winner with his prize—a full bottle of Black Bettie whiskey. With a whoop and a holler, the winning rider rode back to meet a procession coming on foot down the mountain trail. Leading them was the groom himself who was given the first drink from the bottle. Thus fortified, the groom led the procession on to meet his bride, while the winner of the race shared his bottle with his friends before hiding it away in his shirt.

Someone finally thought to claim the preacher to perform the "marrying", and the tavern crowd moved on to the wedding.

The landlord assured Jonathan and Ann they would be welcomed at the festivities. The sounds of merry-making were inviting but the quiet of the deserted tavern was more so. They didn't even mind that the gable ends of their sleeping loft were opened wide to bats and bugs, as they lay close in cherished privacy.

The next day, Jonathan and Ann rode the steep slopes of Chestnut Ridge.

"How ever do the cows keep their footing?" Ann asked as she watched them grazing high above.

"Mountain cows are born with their inside legs shorter so they can stand on a slant," Jonathan teased.

"What if a cow's legs are short on the wrong side?" Ann laughed merrily.

On Meadow Mountain they reached the Continental Divide where all streams divided, some flowing east toward the great Atlantic Ocean and the others through the mountains to the Mississippi River. The road had been built during the Revolution for General Braddock. It bypassed the Cumberland Narrows, but half way through a deep narrow ravine, they met a long pack train coming from the East.

"This is a bad spot for robbers. With only one armed rider for each end of a horse-train, packers have to stay mighty alert. Their goods are valuable transport."

As the pack approached, the rider bawled out in friendly voice, "This gal-danged path's so narrow if you try to ride past you're gonna get bumped. There's fifteen o' the pack horses and the trail here is barely wide enough for their load."

Each riderless horse was heavily loaded with packs. Their cargos spread so wide that they scraped the sides of the ravine as they pulled through the narrow path. The Jennings had to back their horses till they found a place they could wait for the pack to plod by.

"Your mare's a good back-stepper," Jonathan complimented Ann on her handling of Ginger.

"What's in the packs, do you think?" as they waited eating apples from their food pouch.

"Maybe tools, flax, pork—whiskey for sure. Umm-um, these pippin apples are good enough to be from Johnny Appleseed's orchards."

"I hope he finds our Quaker Friends. I'm still carrying his seeds to deliver to Dolley Madison."

"You'd best refer to the wife of the President as Madame Madison."

"Does anyone call her Lady Presidentress?"

Jonathan only shrugged for now the end of the pack train was in sight. They gave the rest of their apples to the rider bringing up the rear.

"I wish we had enough for the horses. They look so sad with just packs and no riders."

123

The trail widened again but it was so isolated that a flock of turkeys walked ahead of them unafraid until they disappeared into the woods. It was close to sunset before they reached a small plateau on Sideling Hill.

"It's beautiful here. Must we move on to a tavern?" Ann was thinking of the public living with the smell of whiskey and the spittle of tobacco. "Please, can't we stay here tonight?"

The sunset had fragmented the sky into a spectacular blaze of color. In the still quiet, they heard the muffled wings of an owl gliding swiftly from its hiding place to silence forever the chatter of a squirrel.

A great orange moon was rising in the darkening sky.

Jonathan held out a crimson leaf, "Indians call this September moon the 'moon-of-the-falling-leaf'."

"I could stay here always," Ann spoke softly. "Is this really our last day in the mountains?"

"We'll stay here tonight," and he hastened to lead the horses to a small pasture the size of a cabin. I'll get our provisions," he called back but Ann had moved away.

He saw her standing free on a ledge with her arms outstretched as if she would hold the beauty of the mountains and valleys in her grasp. Silhouetted against the vastness of sky and tree, she looked small and vulnerable.

Jonathan dropped the leather food pouch beside a fallen log and hurried toward her.

"The pine trees look as close as a woven carpet," Ann greeted him. "If I fell, I bet I'd land soft and plushy."

"You might land on a burr bush again," and he pulled her away from the dangerous ledge. He, too, felt the romance of the view and he took her into his arms, whispering gently into her ear, "Let's eat."

Ann laughed good-naturedly. They retraced their steps but Ann lagged behind, reluctant to leave any part of this mountain magic. Suddenly Jonathan shouted. "It's a bear. Stay still."

Ann saw a black shadow emerge from the far end of a hollow log. Jonathan held his rifle ready but the bear, too, was surprised and he lumbered away in great clumsy strides. Jonathan was satisfied to let him go until he saw that the bear was hugging something in his arms.

"He's got our food pouch. Stop! Stop!" he bellowed as if he were calling to some human thief.

The bear stopped frozen like a picture on a postcard. Then he ran crazily straight toward Ann.

A bear can climb a tree but not a sapling, Ann had been told. She ran for the nearest sapling. Then she hesitated. Would this slender tree hold her? Could she climb in her long riding skirt? The looming bulk drew closer and Ann hesitated no longer.

She vaulted to the first branch like the little monkey had leaped to her shoulder. Her skirt caught on the twigs that crunched under her weight. Her hair lost its pins and the long strands fastened around a branch.

Trembling like the leaves, Ann clung to the tree. The sapling swayed and swung as she tried to climb higher.

At the foot of the sapling, the bear stood bewildered still hugging the food pouch. The bag was dripping with honey, and pork grease was slobbered over its sides. Suddenly the bear turned angrily toward Jonathan. Here was the one who had interrupted his food orgy. The bear moved closer to his enemy.

From her perch on the sapling, Ann saw the great bear turn toward Jonathan and she screamed in terror. Again and again she screamed with hysteria. The bear stopped in confusion. Then he lumbered away crashing clumsily through the trees.

"He's got our food," shouted Jonathan and he pursued the fleeing bear with aimed rifle.

Still in the tree, Ann shook like Johnny Appleseed with the "ager." From the distance came the shattering discharge of a rifle. Then all was silent.

Ann listened desperately. Had Jonathan killed the bear? What if he had only enraged him? Could he re-load his rifle fast enough for another try? A second shot sounded through the woods—then all was still once more.

Ann waited. When she heard nothing more, she slowly and tearfully began to climb down from the shaking sapling. At last she saw Jonathan coming out of the woods. He was staggering.

"O Jonathan, are you hurt?" She moved to embrace him when she saw that he was struggling to hold the stolen food pouch away from his body. It was dripping honey and grease but now it also dripped blood.

125

"I've just shot the biggest four-hundred pound bear I've ever seen. But I had trouble getting our food pouch away from him."

"Why didn't you let him go? He might have killed you!" Ann spoke with a rush of words mixed with anger and relief.

"I shot to scare him into dropping the bag. Then he turned on me, mean. But I re-loaded my rifle in twenty seconds. I once won a competition re-loading a Kentucky rifle. They're made right here in Pennsylvania, you know."

Ann was indignant. "Who cares about the food pouch. We won't be eating victuals from that." She showed her disgust. "And if that bear had reached my skirt as I hung on that tree, he could have snapped the sapling and I could have fallen into his jaws. I could see his great ugly tongue," and she shuddered.

Jonathan was unmoved by her anger. He was feeling good at having killed the bear. "I saved your life, of course. If folks read headlines in the Pittsburgh Gazette, I'll be a hero—'Delegate to Congress from the would-be-state-of-Indiana saves his bride from a big black bear'," he spoke in jest.

"You know perfectly well it was my screaming that saved us both."

Jonathan was still satisfied with his conquest of the bear. "Anything you say, Madame Jennings. The Gazette should print that a lady's screams saved more than her honor."

"Now Jonathan you know it is no laughing matter."

"But it's no matter if you laugh," he replied.

"Why didn't the horses alert us to the bear?"

"I suspect the bear was squeezed into that hollow log when I dropped our food bag there."

"You mean he was hibernating?"

"Old logs are full of bugs and beetles and bears love 'em."

"Not more than honey."

The two looked at each other. Ann had a rent in her skirt and she had lost her hairpins to leave her beautiful hair clinging about her shoulders. Jonathan was in a honeyed, greasy, bloodied state. Suddenly they both began to laugh each pointing to the other's absurd appearance.

"And now we've nothing to eat. There's a tavern at the summit of the mountain if we can make it before dark. I'd best get the horses."

But when Jonathan approached Big Brown, the great horse stomped about and tossed his head, sneezing and bugling through his nose, showing his disapproval of the strange sights and smells.

When they took to the trail, they came to the huge sprawling carcass of the bear. Already insects were at work and a vulture circled overhead.

"Lots of good bear meat going to waste. What would you say to a nice bearskin rug?"

"You can plague a body!" The agitations in Ann's stomach were not from hunger.

The horses stepped skittishly around the dead animal as it almost filled the trail. They began to climb, with the sky almost hidden now by the dark of the forest, but finally they reached the Summit House. The tavern was well-named since it set at the very summit of the mountain but it was only a one-room cabin.

Landlord John Slack greeted them. "You look like you could use a shin's worth of unadulterated whiskey, my travelling friends. It's late to be coming across the mountain."

"We were attacked by a bear," said Ann. Then she noticed Jonathan's expression and she hesitated, "We-l-l, our provisions were." While Jonathan led the horses to the watering trough and tried to wash away some of his own unpleasantness, Ann told their story.

"It's a good thing it wasn't a she-bear with cubs about. But you're in luck this night. We've other travellers stayin' and the Missus is fixing a real feast—roast bear meat."

Ann shivered but she followed the landlord into the small cabin. The entire room seemed to be fireplace. It filled one whole end of the cabin wall.

The taverner tended the huge fire with a seven-foot poker. "Keeper-of-the-poker, I be. I put it under lock and key," he sang out. "Leastways I have to, for it takes a wagon full o' wood to keep this fire going come winter and I don't want none of the folks a wastin' any. Choppin' takes a heap o' back bendin'. Snow gets mighty deep here and the wind blows cold. Here, Lady, you kin be a settin'," he pointed to a barrel, "while the Missus be fixin' your victuals."

When the food was ready the guests ate heartily, smacking their lips over the bear meat. Jonathan pretended not to notice that Ann only picked at hers.

127

"That bear I shot would make elegant eating, John Slack. Why don't you go down the mountain for him? She must be a five-hundred pounder," bragged Jonathan. "He's all yours for the taking."

"Thankee, Mister Jennings. I wager his winter-thick fur would make a fine cover. When you come this way again, we kin use it to keep your Missus warm."

Ann turned away. "Could I be going to the loft now for sleeping?" she asked the landlord's wife. "The day has been long."

"Indeed, Ma'am, the loft is full o' onions and new-dug potatoes fer winter. There ain't room fer sleepin'. You be welcome with the others here by the fire."

The kindly woman held a lantern to lead Ann to the outhouse and Ann stopped at the stable to caress Ginger. She whispered into the little mare's ear. "Why did I ever come on this frightful journey!" Ginger nodded up and down and twitched her ears. "You're right, of course. I came because I love Jonathan. As one lady to another, you are a comfort, my dear Ginger."

Ann and Jonathan slept that night rolled in their blankets spread on the rough wooden floor before the fire along with the other travellers. But even with Jonathan close beside her, Ann slept fitfully. She dreamt that she was falling out of a tree into the arms of a bear that hugged her. As she struggled against the animal, she woke in a sweat to find it was Jonathan thrashing about in his sleep.

"Jonathan, Jonathan, wake up! You're hurting me," as his arm weighed heavy on her. "You're having a nightmare."

"Uh huh," he muttered half awake. "I was dreaming that I was trying to keep you from falling off the mountain into the pine trees. Here," he whispered as he moved closer, "I'll give you a bear hug," and he chuckled.

"Move away, Jonathan, you stink of bear."

"What you smell is a skunk outside the cabin. I trust it won't get near Ginger." With that he turned over and went promptly back to sleep, leaving Ann in a torment of concern.

But dawn arrived finally and an appetizing breakfast of buckwheat cakes made up for meals missed by the now hungry Ann.

"Madame Jennings, will you be choosin' maple sugar or honey for your pancakes?" the landlord's missus asked.

Without waiting for Ann's reply, Jonathan answered sternly, "We'll be having *maple sugar*."

XI

City-Of-No-Houses

A few days later they reached the turnpike where they shared the road with other saddle-horses, wagons, and carriages. Once they passed a stagecoach from the north. Often they had to pull over for a herd of cattle trudging to market with their owner. Ginger whinnied and snorted as she followed steady Big Brown on the natural paths alongside the pike.

"It's so exciting. We must be drawing near to Washington City."

"We'll stay the night in Hyattstown. There's an Ordinary there."

"Is this an Ordinary?" Ann asked when they reached Hyattstown. "Why it's just an overnight tavern."

The landlord heard Ann's question. He was a man of property, the unofficial head of the small village, and he took it upon himself to answer.

"An Ordinary is an inn where prices for accomodations are posted for all to see. This way, you travelling gentlemen—and ladies," he added bowing to Ann, "can't be overcharged."

"Not like the charges at Castleman House back in Grantsville valley," added Jonathan.

"You mean the lady here travelled through the mountains and on horseback. I mean no offense, Madame, but you don't look travel-weary."

"We have come all the way from the Indiana Territory, Sir," Ann spoke proudly.

Others gathered about. "Holy mackerel, Lady, wasn't you scared? Indians and wolves and bears 'n all?"

"You say you come from Indianny?" asked another. "Where's that?"

Jonathan was patient. "It's an important part of the Union, my good man. It's beyond the mountains but it has everything needed for settlers—good soil, water, timber, rivers for grinding grist, good sturdy pioneering people—in fact, it's close to having the quota required for becoming a state."

131

Ann made some excuse to cut Jonathan off. "After all," she said later, "the man only asked where Indiana was. You didn't have to make a speech on its glories."

"We need settlers. When we get a road one day, folks won't be asking where Indiana is."

"I guess some people here in the East will never learn what lies over the mountains."

"All the more reason the country has needs for roads if it's to remain united."

In this part of the country, Ann encountered more ladies travelling, but at an inn they were expected to take their meals in the privacy of their rooms. Ladies were never seen dining in the Commons Room.

"Why then are they called *commons*?" Ann asked sulkily. "Should not the room be common to both gentlemen and ladies? I like the sleeping privacy but I do not like eating alone."

That evening, Jonathan returned to their sleeping room late and he found her waiting up for him.

"Why, you've been crying, Ann."

"I do not like the separation. Eating by myself gives me no appetite."

"You'd best get accustomed to being alone. When we get to Washington, my work will often keep me away from you."

"You're not going to sleep now, are you?" as Jonathan made ready to retire. "I've had no one to talk to all evening."

Jonathan sighed. "I have much to learn about a wife. I've had only political talk—you wouldn't find it interesting."

"It's my country, too."

"All right, my eager wife," and Jonathan lifted Ann lovingly into the slat-backed rocker where he tucked a wool pieced comforter about her knees against the chill of the dying fire.

"I've learned others are pressing for a road all the way to the Mississippi. I met Sam Drake from Kentucky and he tells me that if they don't get a road from the East, there's talk of Kentucky withdrawing from the Union. He tells me that lawmakers should be alarmed for the nation's unity."

Jonathan's voice went on and on. Ann pushed her rocker back and forth against the monotonous creaking of the planked floor.

She was too sleepy to notice when Jonathan carried her tenderly to the high-backed bed. He pulled the coverlet to her chin in the now cold room and stood looking down at her in the soft light of the lamp. Then he lay restlessly beside her, unable to sleep, as he thought of the many problems the Congress would be facing. Could the young country meet them and keep its states united?

Jonathan whispered softly to the sleeping Ann, "There's much ahead to trouble me, but even if I put you to sleep, I like the sharing."

The last day of their journey, they rode into the town of Rockville where they found a room in old Hungerford Tavern.

Ann chattered nervously, "I'm too excited to sleep. All those important people in Washington. I'll be too scared to speak."

"You'll find a way," Jonathan teased but soon he was snoring, adding to the creakings and grindings of the wagons as they rumbled past the tavern over the brick road.

By the next morning, Ann made ready for the last miles of their journey. Remembering the decorated Conestoga horses, she had the stable-groom fasten red rosettes to Ginger's bridle and braid the mare's tail elegantly with shiny red streamers. The little horse seemed to hold her head even higher as she pranced about.

The boy was attempting to trim Big Brown the same way, but the stallion tossed his mane and shook his head up and down.

"What in tarnation are you trying to do to my horse?" Jonathan exclaimed when he saw him. "Be off, boy. Keep those ribbons for some wagon horse—this stallion's a saddler. And Ann, how do you expect the mare to keep flies away with her tail fancied up like that?"

Ann drew herself up indignantly. "You should be satisfied that I'm not riding a jenny-mule into Washington City." But she drooped in disappointment and whispered into Ginger's ear, "You look beautiful and you have to be dressed up for both of us. All I have to wear for my arrival are these tired riding clothes." She sighed. "Dress-up clothes will have to be my first concern." Ginger shook her radiant ribbons as if she understood.

But Ann's spirits recovered quickly in the excitement of the last miles. The sun shone in clear brightness and cast its rays like a spotlight on the far-stretching views of trees and river. Ann stood up in her stirrups. "Are we close? Where is the Capitol Building?"

Jonathan smiled at her eagerness. "We aren't that near. It doesn't stand tall enough to be seen this far away."

"The Capitol Building should stand taller then, for everyone to see."

Following Rock Creek, they came soon to elegant mansions set back in long lanes of elms and oaks like old English manor houses.

"Are these houses to lease?"

Jonathan laughed. "There'll be no such mansions on a Congressman's salary. This is George Town, plantation country. It was settled long before Washington City was declared the new Capital."

They came finally where the road crossed Rock Creek through a covered wooden bridge. Big Brown hesitated at the heavy sound of his own hoofs on the widely-spaced planks over the tumbling waters below. Jonathan applied his crupper lightly and Big Brown moved across.

But Ginger heard the pounding of Big Brown's hoofs on the heavy planks and for the first time, she refused to follow the stallion. At that moment, a heavy wagon rolled across the bridge with a deep rumble that terrified the mare. Ginger spread her four slender legs and stood stock still.

"Ginger's balking," Ann called to Jonathan at the other end of the bridge. "What shall I do?"

"She's acting like the jenny-mule. You knew how to handle the jenny."

Ann tried soft words and gentle strokes, but Ginger was used to those. She was not used to covered bridges with waters rushing beneath, and no kindness could conquer her fear.

In exasperation, Jonathan started to return, but the sounds of Big Brown's hoofs echoing through the bridge further terrified Ginger. She began to whinny and back up with nervous gait.

Ann dismounted then and tried to lead the frightened mare across the planks but Ginger would not budge on to the bridge.

"Leave her behind and cross on foot," Jonathan called. "When she sees that you're going without her, she'll come quick enough."

So Ann ran lightly across the bridge floor. Even her small boots made a hollow sound on the broad planks.

"If Ginger doesn't come mighty quick, I'll put you behind me on Big Brown and we'll ride into Washington."

"O Jonathan—not into the Capital of our country. That would be disgraceful."

Then Ann suddenly saw ahead. There at last lay the city she had travelled so far and so long to see.

"Now you can just see the Capitol Building—way at the end of the road on Jenkins Hill." Jonathan pointed proudly.

Ann stared as if magnetized. She didn't seem to notice that the dirt road stretching before them was as filled with mud and rain puddles as the woods trail they had travelled. Nor did she seem aware that buildings, not yet completed, stood in marshlands and weeds.

Without turning her eyes from the scene before her, Ann spoke softly, "The Capital of my country! It's beautiful, beautiful!"

"Yes, beautiful!" Jonathan, too, spoke softly but he was not looking at the vista of Washington City. He was seeing only Ann's shining face. "And I have brought her here safely." He spoke the words like a prayer.

Jonathan dismounted. "Now can you see the two wings? One is for the Senate and the other," he spoke with pride, "the other wing is for the House where my office will be."

At the other end of the bridge, Ginger still whimpered and fussed. Finally she could stand the separation no longer. With frightened eyes and tossing head, the mare danced across the planks.

As if in a dream, Ann mounted the mare and the riders rode on until they entered the broad avenue. The road seemed to come alive. Forgotten was Ann's apprehension over travel-weary clothes as she tried to look in all directions at once.

She was captured by the fascination of passing carriages and their exquisitely gowned passengers with liveried drivers holding reins in white gloved hands. Distinguished gentlemen sat well on magnificent horses. Beautifully gowned ladies minced along board walks clinging to the arms of their gentlemen who walked protectively next to the street to spare them from mud splatters.

Ladies lifted their long skirts coquettishly to avoid snagging splinters from wooden walkways.

Ann was surprised to see that many passersby recognized her husband. They doffed their fine hats and bowed graciously. Ann and Ginger kept perfect gait, and many a head turned to look after the beautiful young horsewoman who sat so expertly on the parade-stepping mare with red ribbons flying from the bridle.

"We'll pull up here at Tomlinson's Hotel. They may have information on lodgings."

A groom rushed to hold the horses as they dismounted at the upping block. "Jonathan, isn't that Senator Clay we met at the tavern back in Wheeling?"

At that same moment, Henry Clay caught sight of the Jennings. He doffed his great hat and approached them at once. "I'm happy to see you have arrived, my friends."

"Only just now, are you stopping here, Senator Clay?"

"I came to purchase tickets for tonight's Grand Concert. I have moved into Thomas Conrad's Inn. I find it a comfortable boarding house with good food, good wine, and good talk."

"And good stabling?"

Clay nodded. "Those wonderful horses of yours—did they stand the journey well? Why don't you try Conrad's? I understand there are rooms for twenty boarders." He bowed low to Ann. "Perhaps we shall meet there." Replacing his handsome hat, he hurried to his waiting carriage with its richly uniformed driver.

"Why do we not try the inn that Senator Clay recommends?"

"Probably too exclusive. Thomas Jefferson lived there when he was Vice-President. Besides, I never heard of their taking lady boarders."

"Not accept ladies? Not even wives of Congressmen? How hateful!"

"Not many wives accompany their husbands here. But there are other boarding houses. We shall see."

It was true there were other boarding houses but many were already filled with earlier arrivals and some were too remote.

"We'll never find a place. Do let's try the boarding house Senator Clay told us about."

Jonathan could see that Ann was becoming tired. "All right, we'll try Conrad's," and they put their horses into a smart canter back to Pennsylvania Avenue.

"Look, Ann, we've come to the home of the President."

The great house set alone and exclusive, surrounded by broad green turf. Ann gasped with delight. "It looks like a palace."

"Some folks do call it the President's Palace but 'palace' is considered to be too royal a name."

"It's a fairyland palace to me! Am I truly just plain Ann Hay seeing the home of the President of the United States?"

"Not *Ann Hay*!—Madame Jonathan Jennings, wife of the honorable congressman-delegate from the Indiana Territory," he teased.

Ann blushed at her mistake. "And must I address you as Mister Jennings, if that be the custom? Jonathan—Mister Jennings—why can't we deliver Abigail's letter to Madame Madison now? It has been such a long time on the way."

"An excellent idea, Madame Jennings. I'll ride up to the door and present it."

Ann withdrew the letter from her saddle pouch where it had rested so many days. How long ago their visit with the Quaker Friends seemed!

Ginger stood quietly and made no fuss at Big Brown leaving them. Ann watched her husband ride up the drive to the porticoed entrance. What a handsome figure he made as he sat well on his great horse. How proud she felt to be his wife.

She watched a boy run to hold Big Brown as Jonathan dismounted and climbed the steps past the four great pillars to the door. A man-servant came to the door and Jonathan passed Abigail's letter to him. In a few seconds he had returned.

Ann asked anxiously, "Will that servant deliver the letter to Madame Madison? Are you sure he can be trusted? Did he promise?"

Jonathan was amused, but Ann continued with her rapid-fire questioning. "Could you see into the house? What could you see? Did you see the President? I've heard tell there are thirty rooms in the house. Madame Madison is said to be an excellent hostess. Henry Clay says everyone loves her because she loves everybody. Could you see her?"

Jonathan gave her no time to ask more questions. "We must get settled. This session of Congress may be called early because of the threats of war."

"War! With the Indians?"

"More likely with our old enemy, the British."

They took the horses into a canter. Ann already sensed that from now on, she would be sharing her husband with another world—a world she did not know. When Jonathan served his first term in the Congress, he had been lionized by Washington society as a popular young bachelor. Would they welcome him back with a bride?

Suddenly Ann reined her mare.

"Now what?" Jonathan was impatient.

"O Jonathan, our honeymoon-journey is over. I can't tolerate having it come to the end."

Jonathan studied her face and his eyes softened. In spite of curious onlookers who passed on the broad Avenue, he reached out and brought the two horses together. Big Brown and Ginger stood quietly as Jonathan spoke for only Ann to hear.

"It won't be an ending. There will be many 'wondrous beginning days' like Becky calls them."

The great stallion and the little mare carried Jonathan and Ann forward then into new adventures in the City-of-Magnificent-Vistas.

Thomas Conrad, the owner of the boarding house spoke sternly. "I'm sorry, Sir, but I take only gentlemen guests, Congressman Jennings." Then he saw the little bride waiting nearby. She looked confidently toward him and he was unprepared for the radiance of her smile.

"The lady must be a brave one travelling all those dangerous distances to accompany you to Washington, Sir." Conrad sighed. "I don't rightly know what the other gentlemen would say, but for such a courageous young lady, I ought to break my rule." Still he hesitated. Then—"Here, boy, take the Jennings' things to the Thomas Jefferson suite."

But he turned back to Jonathan and spoke sternly again, "Madame Jennings will have to take her meals in her own sitting room. All my boarders are important men, and they'll not like carryin' on table talk and voting caucuses before a lady audience."

"No, Jonathan, no!" Ann protested privately.

"Should we hunt another boarding house then?" he spoke patiently. He did not force her to obey, yet she could see how disappointed he was. The very thought of dining alone made Ann shudder but without another word, she turned to follow the landlord up a beautiful broad stairway.

"This was the home of Thomas Law," Conrad was speaking. "When they made this village the Capital, he was the largest property holder and there were so few houses available that he gave his home to be turned into a boarding house for congressmen seeking temporary quarters for the sessions."

When Conrad opened the door to the suite, Ann forgot her new dignity. She flew across the large parlor to the window, for through the fine lace curtains, she had caught a glimpse of the sparkling waters of the Potomac River.

"How lovely! Like the Ohio back home." Then she quickly recovered behavior proper to the wife of a congressman. She studied the gleam of the elegant mahogany highboys and tables, and the thick rugs spread over polished dark wood floors. She looked appreciatively at the four-poster bed and caught her own image in the long pier glass.

"The rooms are excellent, Mister Conrad. We shall be quite satisfied here," she spoke with dignity.

Conrad could see that Ann was as enchanted with the rooms as he was delighted with her. He knew he was certain to be censured in boarding a lady, but aloud he said, "I'm proud you-all like it, Madame Jennings. I'll send Petunia up to serve you. She's a young one but she knows Washington ways."

Thomas Conrad went down the great stairway, muttering to himself. "It will be bad enough when John Randolph finds I've rented a room to Henry Clay—but a *lady* at Conrad's. . . !"

Jonathan had left to see about stabling the horses when Ann heard a light knock on her door. There stood a little black girl almost as tiny as Ann and about the same age.

"I be Petunia, Ma'am. I come to unpack your purties fer you. Where be your valises, Ma'am?"

Ann showed her the saddlebags. "Where be all your party gowns, Miz Jennyings Ma'am?" she asked eagerly. "I'll put 'em by in the clothes press, Ma'am."

"Thank you, Petunia, but I don't have any gowns." Then seeing the girl's crestfallen look, she hastened to explain. "You see I've come a long way and on horseback, and what you found in my saddlebags was all I could manage." Then Ann remembered Bright Cloud's little packet—"Except my Indian robe here."

Petunia unwrapped the packet. At the sight of the white doeskin robe, the girl drew in her breath, "O Lawdy, Lawdy, Ma'am, I ain't niver seen anything like this. It's the beautifullest gown I ever seed, Miz Jennyings." She stroked the soft delicate skins.

"Take care with it, Petunia. It's a love-gift." And she told the girl the strange story of Scotach and Bright Cloud and the Mare-of-the-Autumn-Moon.

"But I'll be needing dress-up clothes right soon. Maybe you can help me find a dressmaker?"

Petunia drew herself up with rightful respect for this brave lady who had accompanied her husband all the long way to Washington from heaven-knows-where.

"I be proud, Ma'am, to serve you anyways I be allowed."

Ann welcomed the attention of Petunia and someone female to talk with. They were soon chatting together as Petunia filled Ann with stories of Washington City and the other boarders. Even with dining alone, Ann felt sure that she was going to like it at Conrad's boarding house.

"Don't be frettin', Miz Honey. I'll be bringin' your victuals to you and when I does, I'll carry what they's sayin' at the dinin' table," and she giggled like the notes of a high scale.

When Ann ate her first dinner alone in her parlor, she had Petunia move the serving table near the half-opened door where she could hear the voices that drifted up the stairway from the dining room. She detected the low resonant voice of Henry Clay and the generous laugh of her husband. One voice echoed high and shrill but try as she would, Ann could not make out the words of the conversations.

"It's downright aggravating. How could they do this way to a lady!" Ann spoke aloud and she stamped her foot in her annoyance, but no one was around to hear.

A moment later, Petunia entered the room to remove Ann's dinner service. " 'Scuse, Miz Jennings, honey, but I's got sumpthin' to tell you."

"Do speak, Petunia," pleased to have someone to talk to. "What are they saying downstairs?"

"That's what I wants to tell ya, Ma'am. There be a new gentlemun what is friends to you. He argufies with sourcrastic old

Randolph gentlemun as how it's disgracing of the whole Congress fer you to be eatin' all by yourself."

Ann was delighted. "That must be our friend, Senator Clay. What did the others say? Am I still to be banished?"

"I don' know about that banish like you say, Ma'am, but Massa Randolph, he said as how he'd up and move if a lady came to board."

"O drat Mister Randolph. Who is he anyway? Where was Mister Jennings?"

"O Ma'am, they daren't speak thataway afore Massa Jennyings. He be takin' his brandy with the other gentlemun in the parlor. He'll be comin' upstairs right soon now, only" and she whispered close to Ann, "please, Miz Honey, don' be tellin' that I be carryin' tales to you, cause Massa Conrad, he ain't too forgivin'-like if'n he finds out."

That night the last sound that Ann heard in her new home came over the croakings of the frogs in the nearby marshes. It was the cry of the hourly watchman as he moved through the dark street, swinging his lantern into the shadows—"Nine of the clock and all's well."

Was all well? Ann wondered.

XII

Dolley Madison's Levee

The next morning, Jonathan kissed his bride in a tender good-bye but he hurried down the stairway, eager to be off to the Washington world of politics.

"Congressman Jennings, Sir," Conrad called out, "a note has just been delivered from the President's House for Madame Jennings." Conrad sounded impressed.

"From the President's House?"

Jonathan tried to maintain a casual dignity but he bounded back up the stairs with the letter. They read the note together:

> Dear Madame Jennings,
>
> Please forgive the abruptness and informality of this note, but the President and I have extended invitations to a reception for this evening at half after eight and we would be satisfied if you and your husband would favor us with your presence.
>
> I hold myself in great debt to you for your kindness in carrying a most welcome letter from my dear friend, Abigail Evens, and I wish personally to express my thanks. My Quaker Friend speaks so well of you that I eagerly await this meeting. The favor of an answer is requested.
>
> Cordially, Dolley Madison

Jonathan was beaming with pride. "O Jonathan—the wife of the President. What an honor! And we're invited to that beautiful house."

Ann was radiant. She danced and skipped about the room, twirling to her own humming like the gypsy girl of the caravan. Suddenly, her feet stopped in the middle of a caper. Her eyes closed tight. Her smile vanished. "I can't go—I have nothing to wear."

"Not go? To the reception of the President? Nothing to wear? That is ridiculous. There must be shops for ladies in Washington. Have Petunia hire you a carriage and take her with you if you need her to show you about. Ladies dress up for Dolley

143

Madison's "levees", so buy something suitable," Jonathan spoke sternly.

He started out the door. Then he turned back into the room. Ann was standing just as he had left her, stunned and close to tears. He drew her into his arms, "Ann, you will be the most beautiful woman at the Assembly, no matter what you wear and you will be mine. I love you." Then Ann's tears flowed freely.

That was the way Petunia found her. The little servant was wise beyond her years and she assumed direction of Ann's plans at once.

"Can't I ride to the shops on Ginger?"

"No, Ma'am. Miz Jennyings must ride to the shops in a carriage," Petunia replied, eager for the opportunity to ride in a hackney herself. "Thataway you be gettin' more respectable from the shop ladies."

The next thing Ann knew she was riding down Pennsylvania Avenue with Petunia beside her in a hired hackney coach. How jealous Ginger would be, thought Ann, if the little mare could see her place usurped by a hired carriage horse.

"If only I could have brought my marrying dress. Do they really have dresses all ready made up for buying, Petunia? I never heard of such."

Their driver suddenly swerved the hackney to let a gilded carriage pass, with a coachman elegantly outfitted and a lone passenger opulently attired.

"Ain't they the haughty ones!" whispered Petunia. "They's plenty o' space fer passin' on this wide avenoo."

The passenger looked straight ahead. "Who is that high-toned gentleman, Petunia?"

"That's one o' them furriners—embassador most likely. Such as them be uppity folk here in Washington and some of 'em don't speak as good as colored folks."

Petunia was delighted with her new importance. She pointed out the public buildings sandwiched between old mansions. Ann admired the double rows of lombardy poplars that lined the Avenue. "President Jeffason had 'em planted when I was a little girl. They's a fine fer cuttin' 'em fer firewood—*five* dollar!"

When they came to a cluster of small shops, Ann recognized the signs for a tailoring shop and for the shoemaker.

Petunia wrinkled her nose at the smells from a fish shop. "They's got oysters," Petunia informed Ann.

"What are oysters?" Ann asked eager to learn everything about this fascinating city.

"I ain't never allowed an oyster only I seed white folks eat 'em at Massa Conrad's table. Looks like they slip down easy. You'll see."

"But not at Mister Conrad's table," Ann shrugged, reminded of her banishment.

Petunia pointed out Mrs. Milligan's Library, the Book and Lottery Store, and Mr. Cooper's Music Store. She whispered so the driver wouldn't hear, "There's the Tobacco and Snuff Store where folks say the Lady Presidentress buys her snuff," and she giggled.

Ann saw a sign for a cloth merchant's emporium. "Is this where we stop?" she asked anxiously.

"No, Ma'am, that's for buying cloth that needs sewing, but there be a lady come new from Philadelphy selling dresses all made-like. It's told she's got fripperies, too—feathers and reticuley bags and gloves and slippers." Petunia sighed ecstatically, "I like to be seeing such."

"Good heavens, will I have to buy such things, too?"

"Course, I ain't never seed the President's assembles, Miz Jennyings, Ma'am, but I do hear the ladies be much fancied up." Then Petunia lowered her voice, "Not much up top," and she giggled hilariously.

"Whatever are you trying to tell me, Petunia?"

Petunia just pointed against her own flat little chest to an imaginary low-cut neckline and rolled her eyes to the heavens.

Ann tried not to join in Petunia's infectious giggling. She must remember her dignity before the hackney driver. It's not going to be easy being a congressman's wife, Ann was thinking.

Aloud Ann read the sign for *The Washington Bookstore.*

"They got books all over the shop," volunteered Petunia. "They sell 'em."

"I never knew there could be enough books to have a store full. Oh, it's going to be exciting living here, Petunia."

"I wouldn't know about books, Miz Jennyings. Slaves can't read. It ain't allowable to learn."

"Are you a slave, Petunia? Involuntary servitude?"

Petunia sat up very straight. "I be Massa Conrad's house girl," she spoke proudly. "That be the goodest. I ain't never been what you say ser-serv. . ."

Ann was spared the need for explaining when the carriage came to a stop. "We here now, Miz Jennyings. You best tellin' the driver to wait—they be packages fer carryin' mabbee," and she descended elegantly to follow her charge.

They had come to the corner of Market Street and Pennsylvania Avenue where stood an imposing house. It had once set alone on a plantation in the earlier days of this once scraggly village so recently turned into the Capital.

"This be Miz Walker's. She done sell things," announced Petunia, still revelling in her self-importance. She turned the brass bell-handle on the great door and they listened to the sound of it echo through the house. A dark-suited man-servant opened the door, his stiff collar holding his head arrogantly. "Your name, please, Mademoiselle?"

Ann was so intimidated by the man's haughty look, she almost answered Ann *Hay*. "I am Madame Jonathan Jennings and I wish to see about the purchase of a dress—er—gown."

He opened the door to admit her but proceeded to close it on Petunia. When Ann protested, he permitted Petunia to wait in the hall, while he led Ann to a well-furnished parlor. An elegantly gowned and coifed lady was seated at her desk.

When the lady made no move to notice her, Ann asked timidly, "Are you Madame Walker?"

The woman still made no move to rise. "Je suis Madame Flaubert," she said with a French accent and with unbecoming haughtiness. "Madame Walker is in Philadelphia. What may I do for you, ma cherie?" turning back to her accounts.

When Ann stated her request, Madame Flaubert asked disinterestedly, "Who recommended you, my child?"

"Recommended?—Do I have to be recommended to buy a dress? Why, I suppose it's Petunia, the house servant at Conrad's. She brought me here." Then with her courage mounting, "My husband is Congressman Jennings. We've just come from Indiana for the forthcoming session of Congress."

"Congressmen are such temporary residents. That place you named—where did you say it is?" But without waiting for an answer, "Where do you anticipate wearing this gown?" Yet she did not rise from her chair and seemed more interested still in the account book before her.

But now Ann's face glowed with excitement as she told how they had carried the letter to Madame Madison and how she had invited them to the President's Assembly that very evening.

Madame Flaubert rose at once. "Très bien. We shall see. Madame Madison's levees demand the best. Voila! I'll arrange a fitting for you."

"A fitting—but the doings are tonight."

She answered Ann with a flood of French until finally, she said, "Be patient, ma petite, you do not understand, non? My already-mades must be shaped to you, comme ça," and she patted her own shapely figure.

She rang a bell then, and a young woman appeared wearing a black uniform with a lacy white apron the size of a handkerchief. After a conference in French, the maid returned promptly, carrying several dresses of glowing colors in shiny satins and brocades, in velvets and silks, trimmed with laces and braids—so magnificent that Ann wondered how she would ever make a selection.

Madame proceeded to drape dress after dress on Ann's slight figure as she stood before a tall pier glass, but the dresses lapped long over Ann's feet or the sleeves hung off her wrists to her knees. One especially low-cut model lay open all the way to Ann's tiny waist.

"It is indiscreet, Mademoiselle, on one so young. You have the stylish waist but nozzing here," and she pointed to her own buxom parts. "Alas, I can do nozzing for you, my child."

Ann's head was spinning with fatigue and disappointment. She spoke angrily. "I am not a child. I will not be talked to as if I were," drawing her poor maligned figure as tall as it would stretch. "I am the wife of Congressman Jonathan Jennings." As suddenly, her anger crumbled and she asked desperately, "Have you nothing?"

"Nozzing, Mademoiselle. What did you say your name was?"

Ann turned abruptly to leave. Then she recollected the French words the Dufours had taught her. She would show this unfriendly woman that the wife of Congressman Jennings,

147

delegate from the Indiana Territory, could speak French, too. She began, "J'ai un chapeau—that's a hat, I have un cheval—that's a horse. The name of un cheval is Ginger. Merci, *Monsieur*, au revoir. Je vous aime."

Ann curtsied and with her head held high, she swept regally from the room. She was pleased to see in the mirror that Madame Flaubert was standing with her mouth agape.

Petunia was still standing in the hall. When she saw that Ann was disconsolate, she tried to comfort her. "We kin buy cloth at the Emporium, Ma'am, and then there be a seamstresses someways."

"O Petunia, you are kind but the day is half spent. You'd better tell the driver to take me back to Conrad's. I don't know what Mister Jennings will say, but I'll just have to give up the doings."

They rode back quietly, for no matter how hard Petunia tried, she could not distract the subdued Ann. When they reached Conrad's, Petunia said, "I'll fetch you up some tea, Miz Jennyings, honey. It allays makes white folks feel better."

When Ann entered the room, the first thing she saw hanging in the almost empty wardrobe was the lovely Indian robe. The bright-colored beads and embroideries glimmered in the sunlight from the tall windows and the gentle folds of the white doeskin hung soft.

"I wonder," Ann spoke aloud.

A few moments later, when Petunia entered with the tea, Ann was holding the robe against her slender body before the long pier glass.

"O Miz Jennyings, honey, it must be the beautifullest dress of any."

"Petunia, what if I wore it to the doings? This Indian robe was meant for a party and Bright Cloud gave it in love." Ann was speaking half to herself.

"Miz Jennyings, honey, I only knows from watchin' folk, but I knows there be some what likes you and some what don't likes nobody but themselves. But folks do say as how the Lady Presidentress, she likes everybody, no matter what."

"There, I've decided. It's the Lady Presidentress' play-party. If she's a true Quaker Friend like Abigail Evens, she'll have a welcome for me no matter what I wear."

That evening Ann ordered Jonathan to stay out of the dressing room while she prepared for the reception. "I wish to surprise you," she explained.

Petunia brushed Ann's hair till it shone, shining red in the lamplight. They giggled together when Ann told of the brush of the porcupine tail that the Indians had used. Ann chose to match her coiffure to her Indian dress, so Petunia wove silk ribbons through long reddish braids and fastened the beaded Indian headband across her forehead.

"Aren't you ready?" called Jonathan, impatient to see Ann dressed for the party. He was more than curious, for tonight all Washington would be meeting his bride. His own formal clothes for the evening had remained in Washington to await his return.

"One more minute," Ann answered as Petunia slipped the beaded moccasins on Ann's tiny feet. The gypsy girl's golden hoops made bracelets for her wrists. About her throat, Ann fastened the delicate locket with the miniature of her husband. At last, Petunia opened wide the door between the rooms.

Jonathan stood ready with Ann's cloak over his arms. When Ann saw him, dressed in his formal fineries, her heart pumped warm waves through her body. How could this distinguished gentleman with the kindly eyes, have chosen her to be his bride. "O Jonathan, how handsome you look!"

But Jonathan spoke no word. All at once, Ann felt uncertain and afraid. A minute before, she was glowing with anticipation. Why was Jonathan staring so? Was her dress inappropriate? Was he angry with her? Petunia, too, was watching anxiously.

Then suddenly Jonathan crossed the room. He flung the cloak aside and took Ann's two hands in his.

"My dearest wife, you are beautiful. I shall be proud to present my bride tonight," and he took her into his arms. Once again, Ann felt the beads and quills of the Indian robe pressed into her flesh.

Petunia giggled in relief. She slipped unnoticed from the room but there were tears in her eyes as she watched the Jennings enter the carriage that would take them to their first Assembly-reception in Washington City.

Jonathan Jennings, Congressman-delegate from the Indiana Territory, and his wife waited at the door of the East Room of the President's Palace. Ann clung shyly to Jonathan and the bracelets on her arm shook a little.

"Don't be afraid," whispered Jonathan, reaching down to her ear. Suddenly the great doors were opened and Ann quickly forgot herself as she looked upon the enchanting world before her.

For there stretched the drawing-room that Benjamin Latrobe and Dolley Madison had labored to make so beautiful. Yellow satin draperies at the tall windows shone like gold in the light from hundreds of candles in the high crystal chandeliers.

Mirrors over the graceful mantelpieces reflected the dazzling gowns and formal dress of the distinguished guests who moved about the room like the images of a kaleidoscope. Fires against the autumn chill crackled in the four fireplaces but the chattering guests were making their own warmth in the homelike hospitality of President Madison's beloved Dolley.

Never had Ann seen such beautifully gowned women in colors she hadn't known existed. The men, too, were dressed almost as handsomely as her Jonathan and she even saw wigs on men who still clung to old-fashioned ways.

The sounds of talk about the room seemed to come to a gradual lull as the attention of the guests, one by one, was directed to the couple standing at the entrance to the room.

"That's young Jonathan Jennings just arrived," one whispered behind her fan, "but who is he escorting this evening?"

"Haven't you heard?" simpered one of the belles. "He's just one of those dull married men now. That's for sure his little ol' bride, I reckon."

"Married to an Indian?" exclaimed another.

"An Indian with red hair! Don't be stupid, Lisa. You-all should know that no congressman with ambitions would dare to marry with an Indian—not even one from Indiana—where ever that is."

"Why then is she dressed like an Indian?" as the low buzz began to fill the room.

"Who cares! Comin' from the western wilderness, she's most likely not even a lady. I for one shall take no notice of her," pouted Lisa.

"Congressman Jennings had best stayed a bachelor. With such a wife, he'll never be invited anywhere."

"But she *is* beautiful and so young," persisted another.

"If you care for that wide-eyed look," contributed one of Jonathan's former favorite dancing partners.

"Doesn't she have any proper gowns? I declare she's an insult to Madame Madison coming here like that!"

Whispered comments swept through the room until they reached Madame Madison herself.

Dolley Madison turned to see the young bride paused spellbound at the entrance to the room. She raised a gold lorgnette to her eyes and the room was suddenly stilled. Every eye was now on the wife of the President of the United States.

Madame Madison left the President's side to cross the long room slowly as the watching guests cleared the way for her.

Ann saw coming toward her a small buxom woman, dressed in sky blue velvet, with a large embroidered ruff about her neck. On her head, she wore a lace turban of gold cloth with a white feather rising from a jewelled pin. In one hand, she swung an embroidered reticule.

The only sound in all that room came from the tapping of Dolley's slippers as she crossed the polished floor. As Madame Madison drew near, she seemed to hesitate. Then she held out both hands toward Ann in a warm gesture of welcome.

"I am Dolley Madison, my dear. You must be Jonathan's bride and the friend of my dear Abigail." She turned then to Jonathan. "Congressman Jennings, you have broken the heart of every belle in Washington, but you have made a charming choice. I congratulate you."

Ann curtsied as her mother had taught her and she felt the warmth of this wonderful woman reach out to her.

"Come, my child, I want the President to meet you."

Ann hadn't even noticed that this lady called her "*child*." Taking Ann by the hand, Madame Madison and Jonathan Jennings crossed the room together to meet the President of the United States.

"Shucks!" said one jilted belle. "Madame Madison is gracious to just about any old everybody."

XIII

Ann Posts A Letter

A few weeks after her first Assembly, Ann sat at her desk one morning finishing a letter to her mother. She dipped her goose quill often into the glass ink well. She described Madame Madison's "dove" party held for the ladies while the men attended formal dinners. "We were served on beautiful blue china," she wrote, "and I am learning to eat oysters, and vegetables like celery and salsify. Madame Madison (many call her Dolley. Of course I don't, although the ladies say I am her pet) gave out her receipt for her popular seed cake which she served with a dish of tea. Another most unusual concoction is called ice cream and it is spoken about that Thomas Jefferson brought her the receipt from France.

"After charades," she wrote, "guests are expected to entertain. I sang some of the songs you taught me and they were well-received. They asked me to tell the story of the Indian robe which they much admired. I even showed them some Indian dance steps. They are teaching me the steps of the minuet for my very first charity ball next fortnight.

"Madame Madison was delighted with Johnny Appleseed's packet of seeds and she found it hard to believe I had carried them all across the mountains through the forests of Ohio.

"I have new friends I would like to write about—especially Margaret Smith whose husband owns the Washington newspaper called *The National Intelligencer*. She took me to a wonderful dressmaker and helped me to select three new gowns to be made up. They are certain to be fashionable. I did not return to the shop of the French lady. It seems that many heard about my visit to her and found my French words amusing, but Margaret says folks were satisfied that I gave the haughty lady her come-uppance. I need to remember that everything one says or does in Washington is whispered about to ready listeners.

"I wish to inform you that I spent your generous gift of silver for fripperies as you instructed me. I now possess a velvet reticule and gilded slippers with party boots to cover them against the muddy crossings, and gloves from *Paris*. The gloves are so soft, the shop-lady said they would fit into a walnut shell (I didn't try) I do thank you, dear Mama, with kindest affection.

"Jonathan has produced his credentials and taken his seat in the twelfth Congress. He is very dedicated. He and Senator Clay and others from our western country are working hard to get the Congress to appropriate funds for a national road. I also speak of the need for a road when people ask me questions about our journey.

"Jonathan carried his message from Chief Great Horned Owl to the President. President Madison was so impressed with the trust the Indians had placed in Jonathan that he has arranged an appointment with James Monroe, the new Secretary of State. I am proud of my Jonathan J. (I mean, *Mister* Jennings) but the talk here is more of war with the British than of war with Tecumseh's Confederacy of Indians.

"I am happy here at Conrad's if only I didn't have to eat by myself. If I ever meet that John Randolph who moved away because of me (so I hear) I shall make a face behind the exquisite fan that Jonathan gave me.

"I had best mail this at once, for letters are so long on the way. I send much affection to all my brothers and sisters and to dear Becky.

Your ever-loving daughter, Ann Jennings
P.S. I like to practice writing the *Jennings*."

Petunia entered as Ann was sanding her letter and sealing it with wax warmed at the writing candle.

"Petunia, can you imagine what it's like to be able to carry a letter to the new Post Office Building to send all the way to Indiana? Mister Jennings says it will go by stage coach to Wheeling, then down the Ohio River by flat boat, and finally by carrier to Charles Town. Do you know where these places are, Petunia?"

"Laws no, Mistis Jennyings. You sure do be the most travelled lady in all Washington. Will you be wantin' me to take your writin' to that Post Building like you say, Ma'am?" Petunia was eager for an errand with such importance.

"Thank you, Petunia, but Ginger needs exercising. I've been neglecting her. The mud is so deep that it's better for me to ride a hackney when I'm dressed up. Today, I'll wear my riding skirt. It's proven as sturdy as Mama said it would. You may ask the stable boy to bring Ginger round to the door."

Ann sat on her saddle superbly as she and Ginger trotted pleasantly down Pennsylvania Avenue. The refreshing autumn air was welcome after the steamy humidity of late September. Both rider and horse enjoyed an easy canter until they came to a section of the Avenue mired in mud and horse droppings.

As Ann slowed Ginger to a walk, she noticed a man, attended by a black servant, strolling along the wooden sidewalk with his hunting dog. The man wore his hair long, tied back with a ribbon. He was flamboyantly dressed in a blue riding coat with buckskin breeches and high-top boots with spurs. He swung a riding whip in his gloved hand to keep his long-eared hunting hound to heel.

On hearing Ann's approach, the man turned and Ann recognized the boyish face of the eccentric John Randolph. She looked quickly away, but at that instant, the huge hunting dog broke from Randolph's side and tore into the street, yapping at Ginger's feet.

Always dog-shy, Ginger was startled. She raised her forelegs to escape the barking dog and Ann slid out of her saddle onto the muddy street.

John Randolph called his dog back at once and the hound retreated to the sidewalk to the side of his master. Ann was unhurt and she got up quickly, but she was ready to cry with anger and embarrassment.

Remaining on the dry safety of the wooden walk, Randolph raised his penetrating high-pitched voice in exasperation. "Shame on your mare! Why do you tolerate such an untrustworthy animal, my good woman?"

Ann could accept her moment of unlucky horsemanship; she could endure the rude audacity that this gentleman was well-known for; but insults to her beloved Ginger were not to be tolerated.

"It was your malicious dog, Sir, that upset her. My mare is a Morgan horse—not a hunter—they do not care for badly-behaved beasts like yours."

As Ann spoke, Ginger was moving closer to the walk. She twitched her shanks and attempted to stomp the mud from her fetlocks. All at once, Randolph's impeccable breeches and elegant coat were bespattered with dung and dirt.

Randolph stood not much taller than Ann. They stood facing each other now, angry eye to angry eye. Passersby on Capitol Hill were watching. It will be spread all over Washington, Ann was thinking.

They stood without a word, but the longer Ann thought of their ridiculous predicament, she felt her anger fading and she began to laugh. Randolph remained unsmiling.

"I'm sorry, Sir, about your clothing, but you have insulted my horse. Are you not afraid that my husband will challenge you to a duel, Mister Randolph, for insulting my mare?"

John Randolph knew she spoke in jest for duelling had long since been outlawed, but he was surprised. "You know who I am? Who is your husband, my dear child?"

"He is the Honorable Jonathan Jennings of the Twelfth Congress, Delegate from the Indiana Territory. You moved from Mister Conrad's Boarding House because of my unwelcome presence. And I am *not* a *child*," she added.

John Randolph had been raised in Virginia, a cradle of American chivalry, and he was not without gentlemanly polish. He made a gallant bow. "Madame, please accept my humble regrets, but I must protest your accusation. Let me assure you that had I known of the great charm of Congressman Jennings' wife, I would have entertained the delightful opportunity to meet her at Mister Conrad's Boarding House."

"But not at the dining?"

"I have taken lodgings elsewhere, Madame, because I sought more politically compatible company to dine with—congressmen who are not so eager to take us into war. That Henry Clay and the boarders who dine at Conrad's are nicknamed the 'war mess'."

"I share my husband's interest in the service of his country, but I have heard that you, Congressman Randolph, believe ladies are out of place in the political arena. It is said you think ladies should stay in their homes with the children and the servants and their knitting."

"I am aware that talk travels fast in Washington. It would seem that you have heard little good of John Randolph." His voice rose in a question.

Ann's friendly disposition made it impossible for her to hold ill-will for long, especially when Randolph directed his servant to brush dirt from Ginger and the fastidious gentleman himself removed his gloves to assist Ann.

"On the contrary, Congressman Randolph, it is also said that you are the most eloquent speaker in Washington. I have been invited to sit with Madame Madison in the President's gallery, and if you promise not to scold the ladies for being there, I shall look forward to hearing your orations."

Randolph showed much pleasure at the compliment and after he bowed low again, he helped Ann re-mount her mare.

"For my rudeness, I make apology, Madame Jennings—and for my dog."

"Do not make apology to me, Mister Randolph. Seek the pardon of my mare, if you will." Ann patted Ginger and waved a friendly farewell as she rode off.

Soon after Ann's encounter with John Randolph, Henry Clay invited her to attend a session of the Congress. He had been made Speaker of the House as Jonathan had predicted.

"This Session may turn out to be of special interest to you, Madame Jennings," he had said.

This was Ann's first visit to the Congress and she was excited. With her new friend Margaret Smith, she joined a few other ladies on the Floor of the House where they were seated on hard benches. With her skirts carefully spread, Ann sat with her feet crossed at the ankles and her hands resting quietly in her lap. "As ladies are expected to do," Margaret whispered.

As the congressmen entered, Margaret identified them for Ann. "There's Congressman John Randolph coming to his desk. Why he's bowing to you, Ann." She watched Ann nod in response. "Whatever's happened to him? He always ignores lady visitors."

But Ann kept her own counsel. Perhaps news did not travel so fast in the Capital city after all, she was thinking. She quickly forgot John Randolph when Speaker Clay called on the Chaplain for a prayer and the Session of the Congress was opened.

Ann listened attentively as Senator Clay presided over a great amount of business. "Dull, isn't it?" commented Margaret, a frequent visitor to the Sessions.

But before Ann could respond, a young page approached the Speaker. Whispering spread through the room like widening ripples from a pebble cast into a pool.

"I have here a message from the President of the United States," Speaker Clay announced. "The President asks the Congress to approve an appropriation of thirty thousand dollars for the purpose of commencing a national road to go from Cumberland in the State of Maryland to Wheeling of Virginia where it will meet the river travel of the Ohio River."

Immediately, an angry babble of voices swelled through the room. The Speaker pounded his gavel to bring order and proceeded to recognize the Congressman from New York who had been first to jump to his feet.

"Why is this road necessary?" the Congressman challenged belligerently. "That's a mighty substantial sum of the people's tax money."

Few in that room had ever been west of the Alleghenys. A road was being proposed that would run all the way to a great river which they had only heard tell of. Voice after voice denounced spending money for this national road from the civilized East to the undeveloped "western" territories, to a land of ancient trees and Indians.

Others were on their feet now. "The Chair recognizes the Congressman from the Territory of Indiana."

Jonathan Jennings stood before them. "The land of our new country approaching the Mississippi River is hanging to the Republic east of the mountains by a thread. A National Road would secure this west to the east and to the very Union itself. Coming to this session, I rode my horse across wilderness and mountain trails where I met pioneer settlers seeking new land to escape the overworked lands in the East. I encountered wagons and pack trains braving the hazards of mountain trails and forests to transport the many needs to our western settlers. My fellow-countrymen, our western brethren are courageous and hard-working people and they deserve better than abandoned buffalo trails across the wilderness. A National Road will not only strengthen the Union—it will save the Union."

"Hear! Hear!" Jonathan sat down amidst a great outcry. Ann felt a warm surge of pride. Many eyes were turned on her as she sat shyly among the lady visitors.

Others were now vying for recognition from the Chair and the clamour grew.

"No, no—too extravagant!"

"Who would want to leave the East for the western wilderness?"

"Take the road *past* Wheeling!" called a Congressman from Tennessee. "Take it all the way to the Mississip'."

"Aye, aye! Take it to Kentucky."

The debate went on and on, pro and con. Then Ann observed John Randolph stand for recognition from the Chair. At once the room quieted, all attention directed to the spectacular little man whose often-cruel tongue and famous oratory were both feared and respected. It was well-known that he was an enemy to Henry Clay who supported a national road. What would this aristocrat from the prestigious state of Virginia have to say about a road to the west?

Congressman Randolph began to speak. "We hear the need for a national road argued pro and con, ad infinitum. Most gentlemen present have never been beyond the mountains to witness the needs of the settlers of our country's wilderness— needs that must be transported at great peril and costly hazards, through old Indian or buffalo trails and man-made traces, by pack train, barge, and horseback.

"But there are two here today," he continued, "who can bear witness to such needs and such travel. I refer to the courageous young Congressman-delegate, Jonathan Jennings, who dared bring his brave young bride on this perilous journey. To my knowledge, Madame Jennings," bowing to her as he spoke her name, "must be the first lady of quality and stamina to ever have ridden a thousand miles on horseback, across rivers and mountains, through deep forests and Indian camps, to be at the side of her husband while he serves his country in the Congress.

"They have brought us first-hand knowledge of the need for a road to our western country. I say, let the vote be called for. In my turn, I shall vote *aye*."

Randolph sat down abruptly. The great room remained hushed. The Congress was taken by surprise at the brevity of the speech and the simplicity of his oratory and they were amazed to find Randolph on the same side as his bitter enemy, Henry Clay.

Speaker Clay may have been the most surprised but he seized the opportunity. "Is the Congress ready for the question?"

Each Congressman was called on to cast his yea or naye. Some chose to cast their votes with long speeches and fancy words. At long last, the vote was completed and Speaker Clay asked the Clerk to read the record and announce the result.

Ann knew how much the vote meant to Jonathan. She trembled as if she had the ague and she felt like covering her ears when the Clerk rose to speak. Then she heard: "The appropriation is approved."

"Huzza, huzza!" came from the so-called "westerners." Ann and Margaret had to be satisfied only to wave their handkerchiefs to show their delight, as ladies were wont to do.

"It's a beginning," Henry Clay said after the session. "Now if we can just keep the momentum going."

"All the way with Jonathan J.," said John Calhoun as he congratulated him on his speech.

"To gloriana Indiana!" was Jonathan's reply.

XIV

A *Very* Woman

The next evening when the boarders were gathered in the parlor to await the call to dinner, the talk was of the appropriation for the National Road and John Randolph's astonishing speech referring to the Jennings. The story of Madame Jennings' encounter with Randolph had made the rounds of Washington gossip.

Henry Clay was speaking. "I wish I might have been witness to that encounter between Congressman Randolph and Madame Jennings. It must certainly be the first time a lady ever responded with such spirit to his sarcastic wit."

"Indeed, the lady must be truly remarkable to have made such a dangerous journey to come to Washington," said Langdon Clemens. "My dear wife, alas, is not given to travel."

"You speak only of the lady's bravery. It is also spoken that she is well-informed for a lady, and have you noticed her charm?" Congressman Grundy was addressing John Calhoun.

"Since when did a gentleman from Carolina not notice a lady's charm?" he replied bowing.

"It is told that Madame Jennings rode the same horse all the thousand miles. A remarkable horse, crossing the mountains and all those miles of forest and treacherous wilderness," spoke Felix Grundy, the Congressman from Tennessee. "He would be a Tennessee walking horse, I presume."

"It was a *she* Congressman Grundy—from my fair state of Kentucky—fed on our magnificent pastures of blue grass."

The men laughed. Henry Clay spoke again, "The mare and Madame Jennings were *both* good stayers. We enjoyed a chance meeting on our journeys here and I can assure you that both the lady and the horse could have appreciated a road."

James Monroe had been listening with his usual quiet thoughtfulness. When he spoke, all listened.

"It is my considered opinion that we are treating this brave lady with much discourtesy. Here she is, living under the same roof, yet we have excluded her from our dining-table."

"You are right," spoke Clay. "Madame Jennings is young but she is a great lady and it is a disgrace to treat her so."

"A lady present at our common-table!"

"Are you afraid your manners could be lacking, Mister Lowndes?" The men laughed for they all knew how fastidious he was.

"With a lady present at our table, how could we discuss affairs of government?"

"It is said that Madame Jennings is much interested in the affairs of our country. She learned much from her journey here."

"A lady interested in government? Even Dolley Madison doesn't permit serious talk of the business of the state at her delightful soirees and evening levees."

"But Madame Madison is a good listener. Perhaps Madame Jennings, who is said to be much liked, could become a good listener," Lowndes yielded with a sigh.

"But what would be done if we wished to vote an important caucus at the table to determine our stand in the Congress on issues?"

"A caucus—that's the very thing!" exclaimed James Monroe. "Why do we not vote a caucus to determine whether to invite Madame Jennings to join us at our dining?"

"A caucus—that's it!". . . . ."Let's hold a caucus!" was heard on all sides.

All the gentlemen were assembled now, awaiting the call to dinner, except Jonathan Jennings. It was his custom to remain in their suite to keep Ann company until the last minute when the dinner gong was sounded.

"Let Senator Clay conduct the caucus now that he is Speaker of the House," said Congressman Grundy.

"I am too prejudiced for the lovely lady. I propose James Monroe. He is an experienced diplomat and the new Secretary of State."

"All right, Gentlemen," Monroe bowed. "I accept. If there be arguments for the defense, Gentlemen, speak now."

"Much has been said about the lady's bravery and beauty, Sir," said the Congressman from the new state of Ohio, "but I should also like to point out that Madame Jennings is reported to have conducted herself well before the Indians of the Calagawtha Sept. I understand Jennings carried messages to our President from Chief Great Horned Owl himself. It is understood that President Madison is so impressed with Congressman Jennings' rapport with the Shawnee that he is considering him for the commission on Indian affairs."

"Well spoken, Congressman from Ohio. Do I hear words of opposition now, Gentlemen?"

Congressman Lowndes interrupted. "Sir, what if Madame Jennings should refuse our invitation?"

"Are you hoping for her to do so?" said Clemens. "It is likely, for we have been treating her pretty badly. Perhaps she will prefer the dove parties."

From her post at the serving table, Petunia listened and her eyes rolled from one speaker to the other in her eagerness to hear, but she gave no outward sign.

Someone called, "Question! Question!" and James Monroe stepped forward. He spoke formally, "Gentlemen, you have heard the question for the caucus. Please to answer with the usual *aye* or *nay*. Congressman Calhoun?"

"Aye!" resounded across the room.

"Congressman Grundy?"

"Aye!"

"Congressman Clemens?"

"Aye, Aye!"

"Congressman Lowndes?" No answer came. "Congressman Lowndes?" Monroe repeated.

All eyes focused on Lowndes. It was Henry Clay who broke the strained silence. "You recall, Congressman Lowndes, our common-table is nicknamed the *war mess*."

"Come, Clay, I am not to be bullied." Then he laughed. "I just wished to keep you all in suspense. I vote *aye* with the understanding that I have your permission to courteously interrupt the lady if she proves to be a speechifier."

The men laughed but poor Petunia in her corner breathed a quiet sigh of relief.

Even Landlord Conrad was called on for his vote and his face beamed like a proud father as he fairly bellowed "*Aye*."

"Gentlemen," James Monroe spoke just as they heard the sound of the dinner gong. "I'm happy to announce that the caucus is unanimous in favor."

"What was the caucus, Gentlemen?" The men turned to see Jonathan standing at the door. "What is unanimous without my vote?"

"Does the gentleman from the Indiana Territory wish to vote '*nay*'."

"O Massa Monroe, Suh, please, please, Suh, don' be lettin' him, please Massa."

They all turned to Petunia. Mister Conrad was horrified at her outburst and would have ordered her from the room, but Monroe stayed him.

"What's the matter, Petunia?"

"O please, Suh," and she started to cry. "Please don' let Massa Jennyings vote nay. He'll spoil everthing."

The men laughed as Jonathan stood confounded. Monroe dispatched Petunia to carry the invitation to Madame Jennings, while the men began to explain the caucus to the confused Jonathan. When he understood, his face reddened with emotion. "Fellow-Congressmen, you have just held the most important caucus of my career. I thank you," and he bowed.

"Hear, hear!" and they all clapped.

Upstairs Ann heard the unusual noise from below and she thought she heard Jonathan speaking. She could hardly wait for Petunia to bring her the news of what was happening. Then she heard Petunia running up the broad stairway. "O Mistis Jennyings, Mistis Jennyings!" Petunia arrived breathless with the importance of her news.

"Why Petunia, whatever is the matter? And where is my dinner—you do not carry a tray?"

"Mistis Jennyings, Honey, the citingest things as ever happened. The men done vote a caucus on you."

"A caucus—what are you trying to tell me? Calm yourself, Petunia, and begin again."

Petunia took a deep breath, "They's all voted anon-anon-mous to invites you to the table."

"Do you mean *unanimous*? The Congressmen voted unanimous what?" and when Petunia had explained again, "Are you sure?"

Petunia shook her head and crossed her heart. "Sure as sweatin'."

"How fortunate that I wear my best everyday dress but. . ."

"'Scuse, Ma'am, they say the invite was for perm-perman—ever day."

"You mean I am being invited to dine with the gentlemen every evening?"

"And Massa Conrad done sent me to bring you down to the dinin' right off to set at the top of the table. You goin' to be hostest-like, he says."

"With all those important men? Whyever have they invited me?"

"I does declare, Mistis Jennyings, they likes you good. 'N folks is sayin' ez how you got ways like the Lady Presidentress. 'Sides I hear talkin' like they think you be mighty brave lady comin' all the way from that place like you call it."

A mischievous gleam came into Ann's eyes. "What if I refuse their invitation?"

Petunia dropped the brush she was readying to smooth Ann's hair. "O Miz Jennyings, you wouldn't ever do that!"

Ann giggled. "There, Petunia, I am only teasing," and she gave the girl a loving squeeze.

Together they arranged the folds of Ann's new dress and Petunia pinned up a last stray lock of the lovely hair. Ann ran from the room in her eagerness but she paused at the door to blow a kiss to Petunia. With her feet scarcely touching the stair treads, she flew down the steps as she had done on her wedding day.

But when she came to the broad landing, she stopped abruptly. There at the foot of the gracious stairway stood Jonathan, his eyes filled with tenderness and pride. Ann descended the remaining steps sedately with the measured decorum expected of a congressman's wife and a grown-up lady.

Jonathan took her hand and placed it over his arm to escort her proudly to the great dining hall. At the entrance of the elegant room, they stood together as they once had done before Chief Great Horned Owl.

The men rose at once. "We are grateful that you see fit to accept our humble invitation to dine with us." James Monroe did the speaking.

"Indeed," Henry Clay added, "we anticipate that your feminine presence will lead us to gentler ways and mayhaps correct our war-like reputation."

"In keeping with our nickname, we members of the so-called 'war-mess' have sworn to fight a duel for your honor, Madame Jennings," said Calhoun, "or for the honor of your mare."

Ann blushed. She knew then that the story of Ginger's encounter with John Randolph's hunting dog had reached their ears. She curtsied low.

They seated her at the head of the great table. In the glow of the candlelight, Jonathan thought she had never looked more beautiful.

It was Congressman Lowndes who proposed a toast. The men raised their glasses high.

"Gentlemen—to the Queen of Conrad's: to Madame Jonathan Jennings—a *very* woman."

"O Jonathan," Ann whispered softly, "this is truly my favorite 'wondrous beginning day'."

Historical Sequel

Jonathan Jennings went on to become Indiana's first governor after presiding over the convention that wrote a constitution serving the State for over forty years. He was always a popular figure inspiring confidence in all kinds of people. He worked unerringly to get the finances of the State on a sound basis. He served seven terms in the Congress and was a member of the Indian Commission appointed by President Monroe.

His many elected offices on low salary left him poor, but he was a lavish entertainer incurring debts which he was never able to pay. His beloved Ann died childless at the age of thirty-five and although he later remarried, it is said that he never recovered from his great loss.

Ann Jennings remained tireless in sharing Jonathan's campaigns, going with him into the remote areas to learn of the needs of the settlers and often nursing the sick. With her knowledge of Washington ways, she became the warm and able hostess especially admired when she entertained President Monroe on his visit to the little village of Corydon, the State's first Capital. She took on the care of her younger brothers and sisters at the untimely death of her mother and was unable to return to Washington City.

Ann's kindnesses were many and her love so outgoing it was told that at her death a golden light suffused the room.

Photograph by Jeannie Denning.

Eleanor Rice Long—Author, teacher, volunteer, and
beloved citizen; but always a wife and mother first. She
has dedicated nearly half a century of service to her
community of Bloomington, Indiana, and to those
around her. She has served as dean of girls, U.S.O.
Program Director, and along with her husband, Newell,
Professor of Music at Indiana University, has written
pageants and musical shows.